REINVENTING THE OPEN DOOR

Transformational Strategies for Community Colleges

Edited by Gunder Myran

Community College Press®
A division of the American Association of Community Colleges
Washington, DC

The American Association of Community Colleges (AACC) is the primary advocacy organization for the nation's community colleges. The association represents more than 1,200 two-year, associate degree–granting institutions and more than 11 million students. AACC promotes community colleges through five strategic action areas: recognition and advocacy for community colleges; student access, learning, and success; community college leadership development; economic and workforce development; and global and intercultural education. Information about AACC and community colleges may be found at www.aacc.nche.edu.

Cover Design: Larnish & Associates
Interior Design: Brian Gallagher Design
Editor: Deanna D'Errico
Printer: Kirby Lithographic, Inc.

Community College Press
American Association of Community Colleges
One Dupont Circle, NW
Suite 410
Washington, DC 20036

Printed in the United States of America.

Suggested Citation:

Myran, G. (2009). *Reinventing the open door: Transformational strategies for community colleges.* Washington, DC: Community College Press.

Library of Congress Cataloging-in-Publication Data

Reinventing the open door : transformational strategies for community colleges / edited by Gunder Myran.
     p. cm.
  Includes index.
  Summary: "Offers a new, broader model of the open-door philosophy of community colleges to better serve an increasingly diverse student population by not only ensuring access to higher education, but also by ensuring success, a campus environment of inclusiveness, and the colleges' engagement with the communities they serve"—Provided by publisher.
  ISBN 978-0-87117-391-1
  1. Community colleges—United States. 2. Community and school—United States. 3. Underprepared community college students—United States. I. Myran, Gunder A. II. Title.

LB2328.R36 2009
378′.0520973—dc22
                                                      2009049731

REINVENTING THE OPEN DOOR

Transformational Strategies for Community Colleges

Contents

Preface

The publication of *Reinventing the Open Door* had its genesis in 2004 with the creation of the Open Door Project of COMBASE, a national consortium of community colleges dedicated to advancing the community-based dimensions of the community college mission, and Wayne County Community College District (WCCCD), a multicampus district serving Detroit and other Wayne County, Michigan, communities. Both organizations were advocates for new initiatives that would combat threats to the closing of the open door of educational opportunity for low-income groups, minorities, immigrants, and other at-risk populations due to changes in factors such as public policy, federal financial aid, the declining finances of community colleges, accreditation requirements, and the digital divide. The purposes of the Open Door Project were to

- Identify changing practices of community colleges in sustaining the open door of access to higher education and career opportunity.
- Identify practices that maximize student retention and success for underserved and underprepared groups.
- Determine how changes in open-door practices are reflected in the ways open-door strategies are executed, such as policy development, community relations, curriculum development, teaching and learning, faculty and staff development, and financial management.

As a part of the Open Door Project, COMBASE and WCCCD co-sponsored in 2005–2006 a national survey of changing open-door practices in community colleges (Myran & Martinez, 2006). Community college presidents and executives were asked to indicate the degree to which changes in national and state public policy, student diversity, the programs and services of the community college, institutional factors such as finances, and community demographic and economic patterns were driving the reinvention of their colleges' open door. Respondents were also asked to share exemplary practices that they felt were emblematic of an emerging new model of the open door.

The survey revealed that significant changes were indeed occurring in open-door practices, with initiatives having the most impact in areas such as partnerships with public schools, developmental education, services to single parents with small children, community outreach and student recruitment, and modifications of federal financial aid. The survey provided evidence that a new model of the community college open door was emerging; that this new model had the four dimensions of student access, student success, campuswide inclusiveness, and community engagement; and that many community colleges were reinventing the open door through exemplary programs and services that gave expression to these four dimensions.

The national survey of emerging open-door practices was followed by a national conference in Detroit in May 2006. Sponsored by the American Association of Community Colleges (AACC), COMBASE, and WCCCD, the conference brought together representatives from community colleges across the country to share best practices regarding the four emerging dimensions of the new open-door model. The conference provided an opportunity for participants to engage in dialogue about the transformation of curricula, student services, teaching and learning, faculty and staff development, learning technologies, and community outreach that is giving shape and substance to the emerging new model.

THE ROLE OF WCCCD IN THE OPEN-DOOR PROJECT

WCCCD serves 32 communities and townships, including the city of Detroit, which has many challenges. It is one of the most segregated cities in the nation. It has much poverty and crime. Its public schools have one of the highest dropout rates in the nation. Its unemployment rate is among the highest in the country, and its economy is in steady decline, leading to a high rate of home foreclosures and nonpayment of property taxes. The adult illiteracy rate in Wayne County is very high. But in this turbulent setting, WCCCD is a beacon of hope.

In 2002, as a component of its Pathways to the Future initiative, leaders determined that the reinvention of the district's open door would be the leading edge of WCCCD's role in community revitalization and economic recovery. As well, leaders of the district felt that WCCCD was a prototype of the community college of the future in that other colleges would face similar challenges as their constituencies became more diverse and needy. As these colleges faced these challenges, they would become living laboratories for the transformation of the open door. Viewing the reinvention of the open door as a national rather than a local mandate only, WCCCD sought opportunities for shared learning with other community colleges, and ultimately developed the Open Door Project partnership with the COMBASE consortium. Through work on the national survey, the national conference, and *Reinventing the Open Door*, WCCCD leaders have sought to be engaged in a national dialogue to benefit all community colleges while also infusing what has been learned into WCCCD's own continuing transformation.

ABOUT THIS BOOK

Reinventing the Open Door is designed to serve as a practical guide for community college leaders and practitioners as they work to align their programs, services, structures, and processes to meet the demands of their increasingly diverse student bodies and communities. It is also intended for use by community college boards of trustees and graduate students in community college leadership programs. The book is ideal for use in leadership retreats, planning workshops, and other professional development venues.

The first three chapters establish a foundation for understanding the open-door philosophy by defining the dimensions of the emerging model, describing the increasingly diverse constituencies, and presenting the leadership challenges in transforming the open door. The four cornerstones of the new open-door model—student access, student success, campuswide inclusiveness, and community engagement—are treated in depth in separate chapters (4–7). The remaining chapters (8–12) address five issues crucial to advancing the new community college open-door model: student services, technology, workforce education, continuing education, and national leadership.

In a *Chronicle of Higher Education* article titled "Community Colleges at a Crossroads," author J. Evelyn (2004) outlined some of the reasons why community colleges are facing trying times. The article included the following quote from George R. Boggs, president and CEO of AACC: "We are facing some monumental challenges right now, there is no doubt about that. One could say we are at a crossroads. The ways in which we confront some of these challenges may certainly define our institutions for years to come." The alignment of unprecedented challenges has forced the country's 1,200 community and technical colleges to engage in some uncharacteristic soul-searching. Enrollments are up, state financial aid is down, and every year more students show up without college-entry skills. How will community colleges pay the bills? Who will lead them? Is open access, the cornerstone of community colleges, sustainable?

In the early 1990s, noted community college leaders Suanne and John Roueche characterized community colleges as being between a "rock and a hard place" as they coped with the realities of changing demographics, expanding technology, faltering public education systems, and limited budgets. They stated, "Access—the promise of the open door—is more critical than ever, and the specter of access unaccompanied by real opportunity for success looms especially large in the face of the unbelievable diversity of students seeking to enter that door" (Roueche & Roueche, 1993). Based on 25 years of studying community colleges and on a major study of developmental education and open-door programs of 12 community colleges, Roueche and Roueche concluded that success for at-risk students was attainable and sustainable if personal factors such as financial aid and child care were addressed. They concluded that incorporating services to strengthen students' self-esteem, such as placing them in classes in which they have a reasonable chance for success, can have a positive impact. They encouraged colleges to establish attainable skill levels and to evaluate programs on factors such as retention rates, student satisfaction, and success in subsequent classes. So, despite often being in such an untenable position, the community college door can remain open for as long as the colleges adjust to changing external and internal realities. And that is what is again happening today—community colleges are transforming themselves with innovative new practices that will help sustain and advance the open-door philosophy.

Who will lead this transformation? Thomas Jefferson once said that every generation needs a revolution. He meant that each generation must learn anew how to apply democratic principles in their time and place. This is what is happening in community colleges: A new generation of leaders—members of boards of trustees, presidents, faculty members, instructional and student services leaders, continuing education and workforce development officers, and other community college professionals—are rekindling the missionary spirit that has always characterized open-door leaders and advocates. This book is written for that new generation.

REFERENCES

Evelyn, J. (2004, April 30). Community colleges at a crossroads. *Chronicle of Higher Education, 50*(34), p. A27. Retrieved from http://chronicle.com/free/v50/ i34/34a02701.htm

Myran, G., & Martinez, M. (2006). *Summary of results of 2006 national survey on reinventing the community college open door.* Unpublished manuscript.

Roueche, J. E., & Roueche, S. D. (1993). *Between a rock and a hard place: The at-risk student in the open-door college.* Washington, DC: Community College Press.

Acknowledgments

I wish to acknowledge COMBASE, a national community college consortium for the advancement of community-based postsecondary education, for co-sponsoring with Wayne County Community College District (WCCCD) the national survey and the national conference of the Open Door Project. I especially wish to thank the COMBASE Executive Director David Pierce for his support and for participating in the May 2006 national conference.

I wish to acknowledge the support and cooperation of George R. Boggs, president of the American Association of Community Colleges (AACC), in guiding AACC's co-sponsorship of the open-door national conference, and for his participation at the conference. I wish to thank Deanna D'Errico, editor of Community College Press, for her extraordinary support, patience, and advice during the editing of this manuscript. I wish to thank the executive staff at WCCCD for nurturing the idea of a new model of the community college open door and for co-sponsoring the Open Door Project. I express my thanks to Charles Kinsley and Latasha Lane for their expertise and professionalism in providing editorial services. As well, I wish to express my appreciation and thanks to the chapter authors who took time away from their busy schedules to contribute to this book.

Chapter 1

A New Open-Door Model for Community Colleges

Gunder Myran

A small percentage of community college students today fit the mold of the traditional college student: attending college full time directly out of high school, age 18–24, and planning to earn a baccalaureate in 4 years. Most of today's community college students attend part time and balance the role of learner with others such as parent and worker. The majority must overcome financial, economic, and personal barriers to academic and career success. Many are unemployed or high school dropouts. Some were not born in the United States. Others live around the world and attend the community college through distance learning. They are rich and poor, young and old, and of just about every color and background imaginable. While community colleges are committed to serving an increasingly diverse student population, the "institutional soul" of these colleges is their calling to play a liberating role in the lives of those who might otherwise be disenfranchised, unconnected, semiliterate, unskilled, and unemployed. It is this sense of calling, of higher purpose, that gives life to the open door of the community college.

Those of us involved in community college work use the term *open door* in many ways: open-door philosophy, open-door college, open-door mission, open door of educational opportunity, open-door concept, and open access. *Open door* is also closely linked to other commonly used terms such as "democracy's college" and the "people's college." However, the community college open door is most powerfully defined as a set of principles and ideas, a philosophy on which the community college is founded. The open door is not an admissions policy or a set of services but an expression of deeply held convictions about the very nature of the institution. That is why the open door is sometimes referred to as the spirit of the community college. The term *open door* is a condensed expression of the democratic and egalitarian principles on which community colleges are based: the spirit of hope for a better tomorrow for all who seek it; the belief that talent and ambition are very widely distributed in our society and not the province of the elite and privileged few; the faith that people from all walks of life can overcome barriers and achieve great things; the devotion to an inclusive campus environment of acceptance, understanding, and caring; and the commitment to serving as a community-based education resource in addressing problems that create barriers to student success such as poverty, unemployment, racism, drugs, and crime. Undergirded by this spirit of hope and optimism, the community college open door can best be defined as a philosophy founded on the faith that everyone can, through education, achieve their academic, career, and other life goals. It is also an expression of all the ways in which community college professionals value, empower, and motivate students who bring to the college unique racial, ethnic, national, gender, age, socioeconomic, geographic, educational, cultural, religious, physical, lifestyle, and other perspectives.

THE EVOLUTION OF THE OPEN-DOOR PHILOSOPHY

From the beginning of the public community college movement in Joliet, Illinois, in 1901, the principle of universal, low-cost access to education beyond high school was established. The early colleges were generally very small. They often operated as an evening extension of the local high school. Adult students might take English 101 in the same room that they took high school English in a few years earlier, while the instructor may have walked up a flight of stairs to instruct a college course after finishing with his or her high school classes. This hometown version of college enabled many students to prepare for transfer to baccalaureate-granting institutions. These pioneer students were typically involved in liberal arts and pre-professional programs and helped to resolve early issues regarding the transfer of college credits from the junior college to the receiving university. The availability of practical instruction in vocational subjects in these early community colleges also served to expand career opportunities for those who did not aspire to a university education.

Two events occurred in the 1940s that dramatically affected community colleges. With the passage of the GI Bill of Rights in 1944, World War II veterans from every social and economic class flooded campuses and changed the face of all higher education. This was egalitarianism in action on a massive scale. In 1947, a commission established by President Truman, called the President's Commission on Higher Education for American Democracy, started a national trend to rename junior colleges as community colleges. It called for a national network of low-cost, comprehensive colleges to serve the education needs of local communities. This report served as the impetus for rapid expansion throughout the nation. During the 1960s, it was said that a new community college was being established somewhere each week. These twin initiatives of the 1940s played a very significant role in opening the door of educational opportunity throughout the country.

During the 1960s, community colleges experienced major enrollment growth. However, this was also a period of social revolution as Blacks and other minorities demanded equality. With missionary zeal, community colleges opened the door of educational opportunity to groups that had historically been systematically excluded. They became a primary education resource for underserved populations claiming their place in society. Innovations such as storefront counseling centers, tutorial services, financial aid, extension centers, child-care centers, women's resource centers, and developmental education flourished. These innovations and the infusion of new students transformed community colleges from campus-based to community-based institutions responding to the education, social, and economic needs of the communities they served.

Since the 1960s, community colleges have led the democratization of U.S. higher education. In recent years, however, rapidly changing external and internal conditions have forcefully indicated that access is not enough. Government units, accrediting agencies, businesses, and citizens' groups are demanding that colleges and universities be more effective in training a globally competitive workforce, closing the academic achievement gap between minorities and the general population, and meeting other societal needs. To respond to these demands, community colleges are inventing new ways to prepare the most underprepared and underserved groups for success. They are empowering these students to overcome barriers such as limited income, limited literacy and basic job skills, physical limitations, and other personal and family factors.

DIMENSIONS OF THE NEW OPEN-DOOR MODEL

In response to these challenges, a new generation of community college leaders is bringing a heightened level of energy and strategy, and a renewed passion, to creating a transformed open door. A new open-door model is emerging that is transforming all dimensions of these institutions. Table 1.1 summarizes the major dimensions of the new model.

Factors Driving Change

Two major factors that are driving changes in the way open-door principles and beliefs are given concrete expression are increasingly diverse students and environmental factors. The impact of increased diversity is well documented in chapter 2. Changes in demographic, economic, political, and other conditions are forcing community college leaders to develop new strategies that emphasize success as well as access, especially as it relates to groups that are otherwise underprepared for a knowledge-based economy. This dimension of the model is explored in chapters 10 and 11.

Table 1.1 A New Open-Door Model for Community Colleges

Factors Driving Change

Student Diversity Factors	Environmental Factors
• Race and ethnicity • National origin • Gender • Age • Socioeconomic status • Physical capacity • Education background	• Demographic • Economic • Political • Technological • Cultural • Social • Educational

Open-Door Community College Mission Statement

The mission of [Name of Open-Door Community College] is to empower students, businesses, and communities to achieve their goals through excellent and accessible higher education and career advancement programs and services.

Open-Door Cornerstones

Student access	Student success	Campuswide inclusiveness	Community engagement

Strategic Institutional Development

College leadership	Student services	Technology	Workforce education	Career pathways and continuing education	National leadership

Functional Implementation

Instruction	Student Support Services	General
• Career education • University transfer • General education • Developmental education • Continuing education • Supplementary instruction	• Admissions • Orientation • Advising • Course placement • Financial aid • Welcome center • First-year experience • Online services • Diversity program • Education background	• Race and ethnicity • National origin • Gender • Age • Socioeconomic status • Physical capacity • Education background

Open-Door Community College Mission Statement and Cornerstones

Table 1.1 provides an example of a community college mission statement that captures the open-door philosophy. The mission statement expresses in a concise form what the social purpose of the college is or why it exists. Mission statements of community colleges vary greatly because they express how individual colleges view their social purpose in relation to the unique needs of the communities they serve. The example provided in Table 1.1 emphasizes individual goal achievement, empowerment, excellence, and accessibility, thereby articulating some of the primary principles of the open-door philosophy. The four cornerstones of the new open-door model are addressed in individual chapters: student access in chapter 4, student success in chapter 5, campuswide inclusiveness in chapter 6, and community engagement in chapter 7.

Strategic Institutional Development

The principles and beliefs that are the foundation of the open-door philosophy are given life and expression through strategic decisions made and actions taken by community college leaders and other practitioners. Student-centered changes in institutional priorities and strategies in response to the increasing diversity and community demographic and economic trends will be the hallmark of the new generation of leaders who are reinventing the open door. The college president and other executives must lead the full expression of open-door principles and beliefs by serving as advocates and catalysts for the coordination, integration, and improvement of programs and services for increasingly diverse students. Similarly, the college's strategic and annual plans must indicate the priority placed on the transformation of programs and services in response to the evolving education needs of students. Changes in organizational design, staffing patterns, the allocation of financial resources, and the policies of the governing board must all reflect specific responses to changed conditions and trends and to open-door principles and beliefs.

The college's definition of effectiveness and its continuous improvement processes must include a focus on institutional improvement and development that transforms programs, services, and processes to better serve the diverse students. Community colleges must also serve as external advocates for diverse students by engaging with community partners in addressing the social, cultural, and economic problems that create barriers to success. And they must be engaged beyond their own institutions and communities to influence state and national public policy as well. Several chapters address major areas of strategic institutional development: leadership in chapter 3, student services in chapter 8, technology in chapter 9, workforce education in chapter 10, and career pathways and continuing education in chapter 11.

Functional Implementation

Decisions about the strategic development of the community college that give current expression to open-door principles and beliefs are executed at the various functional levels of the college. Instructional elements such as career education, university transfer, developmental education, continuing education, workforce and job skills training, adult education, and high school completion programs are at the center of the education enterprise. The success of students from diverse backgrounds depends on how responsive the faculty and academic leaders are to their needs.

In a single class, a faculty member may have many different kinds of students: those for whom English is not their first language; some with physical limitations, others with limited literacy skills. Students may have emotional problems, child-care demands, or other family circumstances that affect their attendance. As if the challenges of serving this diverse class were not enough, this same faculty member must also be more accountable for improving learning outcomes. This type of classroom dilemma calls for increased institutional support of teachers and learners alike, including revised approaches to course placement, expanded and improved developmental education programming, supplemental instruction and other forms of classroom support, innovative uses of learning technologies, interdisciplinary programming, and expanded special needs services. The reinvention of student services will also address many of the barriers to student access and success. Transformational changes are needed, and are taking place, in services such as financial aid, tutorial services, career and academic counseling, testing and course placement, class registration, study skills services, veterans' services, and special needs services.

In addition, faculty and staff members may benefit from professional development programs that nurture new awareness, attitudes, and skills needed to effectively serve increasingly diverse students. Information and learning technologies must adjust to match the readiness and access needs of new student constituencies. Financial planning must recognize the realities of the budgetary demands of changing programs and services. In essence, a commitment to meeting the educational needs of a highly diverse student body must drive transformation of all elements of the community college.

THE FOUR OPEN-DOOR CORNERSTONES

Student Access

Historically, access has been central to the open-door philosophy, and overcoming the access gaps between rich and poor continues be a vital dimension of the open-door model. The majority of students are dealing with risk factors such as limited income, lack of literacy and job skills, family problems, and physical limitations. For example, the low rate of high school completion by Hispanic students, the fastest-growing population group in the United States, presents a special challenge because they and other minorities must ultimately replace aging baby boomers, the best-educated generation in U.S. history, in the workforce.

Community colleges are challenged to effectively serve special groups such as people with mental health problems, high school dropouts, ex-inmates, alienated young urban Black men, and military veterans. Most people in these groups are first-generation college goers who are less likely than traditional students to have a supportive family and neighborhood environment. The new open-door model must emphasize solutions that deal effectively with institutional factors that affect accessibility and the equity agenda of the community college. Examples include the following:

- Proactive efforts to reach out to potential students, schools, and other community groups to instill awareness of the benefits of the community college.
- Creating student-friendly admission, orientation, financial aid, and other entry processes.
- Creating a match between the educational and support needs of each constituency and the programs, services, and resources of the college so that the benefits of enrollment overcome the personal factors that represent barriers to access or achievement.

Student Success

Access alone, unaccompanied by real opportunity for success, is not enough. Adding the element of student success to the open-door model has been a major development in community colleges during the past two decades, although being truly evaluative about the degree to which student learning outcomes match stated education goals is still a work in progress. Community colleges also have a long way to go to fully achieve a student success agenda. Degree completion rates are very low, especially for minorities, single women with children, older learners, and nondegree enrollees. Regional accrediting bodies, pushed by a federal government frustrated by wasted financial aid, have shifted accreditation criteria to emphasize evidence of student learning. It could be said that the future success of the community college itself is dependent on dramatic improvement in the student success element of the new open-door model. Three examples of ensuring success are

- Partnering with students to empower them to achieve their academic and career goals.
- Assessing the effectiveness of programs, disciplines, and institutions.
- Integrating assessment and continuous quality improvement into the organizational culture.

Campuswide Inclusiveness

Because of the increasing diversity among students, community colleges must make a stronger commitment to creating an inclusive and nurturing environment in which students, faculty, and staff work together to create an affirming and open environment in which each individual can grow. In such a setting, those in the college community can learn to see the world through many eyes, break away from stereotypic and dysfunctional ways of relating, and learn problem-solving skills they will need in a global society. The term *campuswide inclusiveness* has been chosen to communicate a concept that encompasses diversity programs, equity programs, multicultural programs, and other institutional initiatives to foster a sense of community among diverse students, faculty, and staff. Campus inclusiveness means fostering

- The expansion of diversity, equity, and multicultural programs.
- A campus environment of acceptance and affirmation in which diverse people can give expression to their unique identities and education goals and a shared sense of common purpose based on learning together how to live in a multicultural global society.
- Diversity training for faculty and staff and for student leadership groups.

Community Engagement

Community colleges are also renewing efforts to confront the very community problems that cause barriers to student success, especially for low-income and minority students (e.g., unemployment, poverty, crime, drugs, and neighborhood decay). This element of the new open-door model is called community engagement to convey the importance of enlisting the involvement of community organizations— economic development and business groups, secondary schools, government agencies, churches, nonprofit organizations, and other groups—in achieving improvements in community conditions and thereby reducing barriers to academic and career success for students. To reach community engagement goals, community colleges are sponsoring

- Service learning programs, community internship and work-study experiences, and other forms of community volunteerism.
- Community problem-solving projects in partnership with other community organizations.
- Community summits and workshops on major community issues such as public school reform, the future workforce, and adult illiteracy.

EVIDENCE OF TRANSFORMATION

Throughout this book, examples are provided of steps being taken by community colleges to give contemporary expression to the open-door philosophy. As an introduction, some of the most dramatic evidence of transformation are as follows.

- **New forms of student access.** Community colleges are reaching into the public schools to introduce middle- and high school students to the opportunities available to them. They are working with high school faculty and staff to increase awareness of literacy requirements necessary to success, and they are involved in revamping curricula at both levels to create a smoother transition. The colleges are conducting special recruitment programs for minorities and other underrepresented groups and providing online admissions, financial aid, and orientation services.

- **On-demand delivery of instructional services and programs.** Increasingly, students expect convenient and high-quality services on demand—when, where, and in the form that best suits them. In many community colleges, online services and programs are the fastest-growing dimension of the institution.

- **Aligning outcomes of programs with the goals of students.** Accrediting agencies, the federal government, business organizations, and students themselves are demanding that college programs produce results that justify the investment. As a result, community colleges are creating institutional effectiveness programs and involving faculty and staff members in ongoing assessment of student learning outcomes and performance-based continuous improvement. The traditional emphasis on the teacher, the prescribed curriculum, the class schedule, and other trappings of academia is shifting to an emphasis on the learner and outcomes of learning (student retention and success rather than "seat time"). The value of a college education is increasingly measured by the success of students after attendance or graduation (securing meaningful employment, career progression, transferring to a baccalaureate institution, etc.).

- **Renewed emphasis on developmental education.** Because the majority of students entering a community college require some remedial education (e.g., math, writing, reading, computer, or study skills), success in adult education and developmental education programs is essential. However, this has been an area of weakness for many community colleges. Colleges participating in the national Achieving the Dream initiative are leading this transformation by placing emphasis on increasing student success in developmental education courses and in subsequent college-level courses.

- **Increased enrollment of older students in career education and the shift of younger students from career education to university-transfer programs that lead to a professional career.** The majority of community college students have the goal of getting a good job and advancing in their careers. For older students who are underemployed, recently laid off, or stuck in dead-end jobs, this goal is very immediate and practical—they want a decent job with security so they can support their families. Younger students see a baccalaureate as a way to ensure longer-term career success, more income, and greater job security.

- **Increased dual enrollments.** Many states now support financially the dual enrollment of students in high school and community college. For small high schools in rural areas, dual enrollment permits the use of community colleges to expand math, science, engineering, and technology offerings. Dual enrollment also permits the community college to help students make the transition from high school to college when they might otherwise drop out or lack the confidence to undertake a college program.

- **Emergence of boundaryless colleges**. U.S. community colleges provide online instruction (as well as admissions, orientation, class scheduling, and other student services) across the globe to students including military personnel, people on business travel, and natives of other countries.

- **Introduction of diversity, multicultural, and other programs to promote inclusiveness**. Community colleges are introducing diversity or multicultural courses and programs; special multicultural events; clubs for racial, ethnic, and national groups; and diversity training for faculty and staff.

- **Rapid growth of learning technologies.** Learning technologies are making worldwide knowledge and intellectual resources available to students and faculty members. Classroom and laboratory technologies are changing methods of teaching and learning, and distance-learning technologies are expanding the reach of colleges to students around the globe.

- **Increasing numbers of "digital natives."** Technology-savvy students are demanding new forms of connectivity from community colleges that align to new forms of online communication including social networking (e.g., Facebook and YouTube), text messaging, e-mail, and personal Web sites.

- **Increased effort to project higher education as a public good as well as an individual benefit**. Taxpayers and government officials tend to think of higher education as an individual benefit rather than a contributor to the public good. As a result, community college leaders are rethinking their engagement in their communities' problem solving and are articulating the benefits of the college to the community through public relations initiatives.

- **New emphasis on assessment of institutional effectiveness**. In parallel with emphasis on the assessment of student learning outcomes, community colleges must demonstrate to regional accrediting agencies and government bodies that they are continuously improving programs, services, structures, and processes based on data derived from the assessment of student, business, and community satisfaction and success.

An emerging generation of community college leaders is forging a new definition of the community college open door, giving renewed expression to the democratic and egalitarian principles on which community colleges are founded. By the strategic decisions they make and the actions they take, they will shape the future of the community college and its underlying open-door philosophy for decades to come. The capacity of community colleges to respond effectively to the challenges they face is questioned in some higher education forums. In an article in the *Chronicle of Higher Education,* Gordon Davies (2007), former director of Virginia's State Council of Higher Education, advocated a new college that he called "the poor college" (based on a passage in Virginia Woolf's book, *The Three Guineas*). Davies argued that because of the widening gap between the rich and poor in the United States, it is time to create a new college that is willing to define excellence as meeting the needs of the poorest among us and guaranteeing them advanced education. He then discounted the will and capacity of community colleges to step up to this challenge: "Community colleges might assume that they fill this role, but most do not. They are becoming more expensive, sometimes for reasons beyond their control. Beset by increasing demand and beguiled by status, many are becoming more selective. Most provide access to the less well to do, but not to the poorest among us" (Davies, 2007).

Davies' challenge may disturb community college leaders, but it must be taken seriously. Community colleges must redouble their efforts to demonstrate the passion, the "fire in the belly," to be a primary education resource and advocate for the poorest and disenfranchised. Community colleges must continue to be engaged with other progressive institutions and groups to build on the democratic gains of the past in areas such as civil rights, federal and state student financial aid, affirmative action, and the rights of people with physical limitations.

It has been said that every society needs its prophets, those who articulate a compelling vision, who call us to greatness and inspire us to action. Every society also needs its builders and carpenters who give life and shape to the vision. Our prophets are the founders of our country, those pioneers who dreamed of a society based on the democratic ideals of freedom, justice, and equality. We in community colleges are among the builders and carpenters; it is our calling to give life and shape to the dream of a society based on these democratic ideals.

REFERENCES

Davies, G. K. (2007, May 4). Accreditation to the people. *The Chronicle of Higher Education, LIII,* 35.

Chapter 2

Addressing the Needs of Diverse Students

Debraha Watson

Traditional perspectives of diversity are reflected in Merriam-Webster's definition of diversity as "the inclusion of diverse people (as people of different races or cultures) in a group or organization." Conversations about diversity in higher education, however, have become increasingly complex in recent years, especially when describing community college students. Contemporary perspectives on diversity in community colleges include a wide array of demographic and situational characteristics of the general population, such as gender, sexual orientation, religion, physical and mental ability, family history of college attendance, academic intentions, academic preparation, marital status, veteran status, parental status, motivational level, socioeconomic background, learning style, part-time versus full-time enrollment status, commitments and obligations outside the college, and English-speaking ability (Ender, Chand, & Thornton, 1996).

Students are attracted to community colleges not only as pathways to 4-year colleges and universities but also for their vocational preparation, adult education, remedial schooling, and career enhancement programs. In addition, community colleges are often more affordable and accessible than 4-year colleges and universities. They offer many evening and weekend classes, willingly accept part-time students, provide outreach services in neighborhood extension centers, and have an open admissions policy.

As open-door colleges, community colleges must address the diverse needs of students as a central part of their mission. The community college agenda is driven by the critical need to retrain and retool the labor force in an economy that has rapidly shifted from manufacturing to technology. Schools must therefore recognize and accommodate the circumstances of students. The primary purpose of this chapter is to examine the broadening definition of diversity and move beyond restrictive historical definitions and conceptual frameworks to create new ways of teaching, learning, and providing broad-based support to students.

DEMOGRAPHICS OF COMMUNITY COLLEGE STUDENTS

Whether one looks at the demographic evidence contained in education research and policy briefs or steps onto any of the nation's 1,200 community college campuses, two characteristics stand out: Community college students represent many distinct racial and ethnic groups, and they are seeking out community colleges in greater numbers to get an education, earn a certificate or associate degree, enhance their job skills, prepare for transfer, or improve their English or basic literacy skills (Laden, 2004). The number of racial minority students attending community colleges has increased substantially in the past 20 years. In 1976, minority enrollment accounted for less than 20% of the total student population; 10% were Black, 4% were Hispanic, and another 4% were Asian American (Snyder, Tan, & Hoffman 2006). By fall 2004, however, the total number of minority students enrolled at 2-year public colleges had jumped to 36% of the total, including 13% Black, 15% Hispanic, and 7% Asian American students.

These statistics support what community college educators already know: Racial and ethnic minority students have a growing visibility on most campuses, establishing this population as an emerging majority. Examining other demographic trends, Snyder and Hoffman (2002) revealed that women in all racial groups continue to constitute more than half of all community college students. In addition, more than 34% of these women students are responsible for dependent children, and of these, 16% are single parents.

As a direct result of the tremendous diversity represented by community college students, complex challenges and opportunities arise for both student and academic affairs. Culp and Helfgot (1998) noted that the arrival of increasing numbers of diverse students represents a "continuing wave of the underprepared, the under-represented, the underachieving, and the underclass." Community colleges must recognize that not all students share the same needs, concerns, expectations, and aspirations.

CHARACTERISTICS OF AT-RISK STUDENTS

Challenges arise for many community colleges because the students they serve are often labeled "at risk." This term encompasses a wide range of problems:

- Entering college academically underprepared.

- Working more than 30 hours a week.
- Lacking financial support.
- Lacking social support.
- Being first-generation college attendees.
- Having expectations of failure (see, e.g., Ortiz, 2004; Roueche & Roueche, 1993; Terenzini, Cabrera, & Bernal, 2001; Yeh, 2002).

In a 1992 National Center for Education Statistics study, authors Kaufman and Bradby provided data from research on the progress of high school graduates through college enrollment. They sought to identify at-risk students and the traits or environmental factors that promoted resiliency despite the obvious disadvantages. Controlling for race and ethnicity, Chen and Kaufman (1997) identified five risk factors. Students were considered at risk if they fit one or more of the following criteria: low socioeconomic level, member of a single-parent family, older sibling who dropped out of school, changed schools two or more times, average grades of *C* or lower from sixth through eighth grades, or had repeated a grade.

Not surprisingly, at-risk students are at high risk of academic failure because they are less academically prepared and more socially deprived. They also tend to be unrealistic goal setters who are largely motivated by the need for instant gratification. Chen and Kaufman (1997) found that those identified as at-risk students in high school remained at risk when seeking entry into postsecondary institutions. They showed that, by 10th grade, at-risk students were less likely than others to have aspirations to attend college, to be academically prepared, to take college entrance exams, and, even if they took those exams, to apply for admission to 4-year colleges. Furthermore, those who enrolled in colleges and universities were less likely to exhibit behaviors of constructive persistence, such as completing remedial courses or seeking assistance with college application processes. They also tended to have an imbalance or low level of peer and parental involvement in their education.

Seligman (1975) used the term *learned helplessness* to describe those with an extreme external locus of control who believe that they have no influence over their own destiny, resulting in a lack of confidence and autonomy. Grimes (1997) noted that some students' attribution of locus of control is a self-defense mechanism by which they perceive positive outcomes as internal and negative outcomes as external. Seligman (1975), Roueche and Roueche (1993), and Grimes (1997) argued that a weak self-concept coupled with prior school experiences can result in students being wary of their academic surroundings. The student's disbelief in his or her own ability can lead to a self-fulfilling prophecy of failure. This failure is observable in behavior such as consistently not bringing necessary supplies or resources, regularly not completing assignments, expressing hostility toward peers and instructors, or conversely, refraining from class participation entirely. The authors concluded that, unlike other students, those who are at risk might set unrealistic goals and be motivated by a fear of failure that is commonly influenced by harsh economic conditions in their home communities. This weak self-concept is the source of most resistance to developing a learning experience that promotes active engagement.

NONTRADITIONAL STUDENTS

The numbers of older, first-generation, and immigrant students have increased dramatically (Coley, 2000; Ryan, 2003). These adult learners with multiple roles and responsibilities are attracted to the 2-year college environment in part because the schools offer flexibility while accommodating their needs by offering evening and weekend courses as well as full- or part-time enrollment. Interrelated demographic shifts, stagnant economic levels, and longer life expectancies have accounted for substantial numbers of returning or first-time mature students (ages 25 to older than 90) to community colleges. Eisen (2005) showed that these non–traditional-age students view their education as an opportunity for self-discovery and empowerment and as a means to improve adaptability to their environment. In addition, many older adults who cannot afford to retire or who have been victims of corporate downsizing and restructuring are now left to refine existing skills or acquire new ones—especially in the area of technology (Laanan, 2003).

This group often faces the same challenges of at-risk students as well as a set of challenges unique to their age and stage of life. Findings indicate that older students and career-changers experience psychological transformation such as anxiety, guilt, and fear upon returning to the classroom (Laanan, 2003). It is normally assumed that, as people age, they will prepare for retirement rather than continuing to work and learn out of necessity. However, rapid changes in technology and other socioeconomic factors can force older adults to acquire new skills or update existing skills to remain self-sufficient.

As adults mature, they are more self-directed and motivated to achieve their academic goals (Merriam, 2001). Therefore, the effect of aging on the adult learner and the implications for learning and support systems must be a priority for educators striving to serve those with hearing loss, decreased cognitive processes, and weakened vision. Furthermore, these students frequently experience an added academic and social barrier because they might be older than faculty members and other students in the classroom.

EMERGING MAJORITY GROUPS

Historically, researchers have sought to classify community college students by gender, ethnic minority, and level of academic preparedness. Although the results have yielded pertinent information for program development and assessments, these classifications often intersect. This makes it difficult to determine which factor places the student at risk. Although minority status is not necessarily synonymous with academic or economic disadvantage, minorities are more likely to be from lower socioeconomic backgrounds and education levels. Ethnic students, however, are not monolithic. Diversity among minority groups exists politically, socially, and economically. All of these factors can affect the student's motivation and ability to succeed in higher education.

Hispanic Students

Over the past two decades, Hispanic college student enrollments in community colleges have steadily increased. More than 55% of all Hispanic students who enroll in higher education after high school choose to enroll at community colleges (Wilds & Wilson, 1998). Despite the surge in enrollment, this group remains notably underrepresented at all levels of higher education; it also has one of the lowest overall education attainment rates of any ethnic or racial group (U.S. Census Bureau, 2000). Nonetheless, the community college has become a critical pathway to higher education for Hispanic students, who are more likely than those from other racial or ethnic groups to begin their postsecondary education at a community college (Adelman, 2005).

For Hispanic students, the decision to attend a community college is often the most sensible choice for the same common and practical reasons that any student might choose to attend a community college. However, some additional factors—such as socioeconomic status, prior academic achievement, and degree objectives—influence this decision for Hispanic students. Hispanic adults have an extraordinarily high labor force participation rate because contributing to the household expenses is a common necessity in most Hispanic households (Fry, 2002). Hispanic women face additional cultural stressors in navigating the higher education pipeline, as entrenched gender roles in Hispanic families can inhibit their education and career aspirations (Rendon, 1992; Romo, 1998). Nevertheless, Hispanic women are more likely than their male counterparts to participate in higher education (Harvey, 2002).

Furthermore, the older Hispanic students are when they enter higher education, the more likely they will enroll in a community college. A substantial portion of the Hispanic community college population is made up of students older than 24 (Fry, 2002). A strong commitment to work and family does not prevent Hispanic students from attaining postsecondary education, although a sense of these responsibilities coupled with low-income status might help to explain why so many attend affordable and conveniently located community colleges on a part-time basis (Fry, 2002). Ultimately, cultural validation is crucial to increasing the persistence and transfer rates among all Hispanic students in community colleges, and any interventions targeting this population must incorporate cultural awareness (Laden, 1998).

Black Students

Researchers agree that Black students have historically been—and still are—underrepresented in higher education in the United States. In response, community colleges have been systematic in providing access to minorities. Cohen and Brawer (2003) noted that Black student enrollment in community colleges in the United States exceeds that population's demographic proportion, as reported in 18 states. However, some argue that community colleges actually hinder minority students from attending 4-year colleges and universities by enrolling them into career and vocational offerings rather than academic and transfer programs (Brint & Karabel, 1989; Nora, 2000; Zwerling, 1986).

First-Generation Students

First-generation college students whose parents have never attended college fall within the at-risk category and often face several barriers when entering postsecondary education. Research suggests that, compared to their peers, first-generation students are at a disadvantage when it comes to basic knowledge about postsecondary education. These students are more likely to face challenges in areas such as financial and family support, degree expectations, and academic preparedness (Pascarella, Wolniak, & Pierson, 2003). First-generation college students have more problems transitioning from high school to college than do other students. According to Snyder and Tan (2005), about 43% of first-generation college students will leave without a degree. These students encounter some of the same difficulties as those whose parents attended college, but often their experiences are exacerbated due to cultural, social, and academic differences. For instance, they are more likely to face financial and academic difficulties due to a lack of access to education opportunities that are generally more readily available to the children of better-educated parents.

Students With Disabilities

Prentice (2002) stated that people with disabilities constitute the largest minority group in the United States. These people were traditionally seen as doomed to a life of economic disadvantage, unemployment, and limited access to education. Students with disabilities are now more likely to be viewed as having the potential to be educated and employed and to lead viable, productive lives. Today, people with disabilities, their parents, and their educators are likely to regard college as a realistic opportunity to gain the skills necessary for self-sufficiency.

Proctor (2001) noted that students who have learning disabilities are appearing in increasing numbers on college and university campuses. It has been reported that, of all students with disabilities, 41% are diagnosed with learning disabilities—a substantial increase from 10 years ago when students with learning disabilities accounted for only 25% of the total. Hawke (2004) concurred, observing that community colleges, with their open-door admission policies and extensive special support services, not only serve the greatest number of students with special needs but also deal with a broader range of disabilities and serve students who are also older than the average. Several factors are responsible for the increasing enrollment of this student population. These factors include early identification of students with learning disabilities, improved services in the K–12 system, enhanced technology, advocacy for those with disabilities, increased awareness of disabilities in postsecondary education, and legislation (Hawke, 2004; Norton & Field, 1998; Proctor, 2001).

Several legislative actions served as catalysts for the burgeoning enrollment of students with disabilities on community college campuses: the Rehabilitation Act of 1973; Public Law 94-142, the Education for All Handicapped Children Act; the Americans with Disabilities Act of 1990, which expanded the Rehabilitation Act of 1973; and the Individuals with Disabilities Education Act of 1990 (including the 1997 amendments). Among other things, these laws prohibit schools from discriminating against students with disabilities. They cover the rights of students with disabilities until they graduate high school or reach age 21.

Under the latter mandate, students are entitled to modifications, accommodations, and services, as outlined in an individualized education plan. Although it is geared toward high school students with disabilities, colleges and universities must be aware of this act because of dual enrollment and recruitment efforts (Hawke, 2004; Taylor, 2004). The Americans with Disabilities Act prohibits discrimination against children and adults with disabilities. It requires all public schools, testing centers, licensing agencies, and most private schools and colleges to allow equal access for those with disabilities (Gregg, Johnson, & McKinley, 1996; Gregg & Scott, 2000).

Overall, students with disabilities have a greater presence in community colleges. However, barriers to access and participation still remain, especially for those with complex support needs. To receive appropriate services and accommodations, students are responsible for disclosing the nature of their disabilities and describing how they might hinder their academic success. To request accommodations, they must provide documented evidence from a medical professional, verifying the disability and recommending specific accommodations (Latham 2001; Lynch & Gussel, 1996). Research indicates that accommodations and modifications fall into three categories: environmental, equipment, and procedural. Examples of these accommodations include auxiliary aids such as books on tape, readers, note takers and transcribers, additional test-taking time or alternative test formats, substitutions for required courses, and modifications in delivery of instruction (Gregg et al., 1996).

Although most community colleges do not offer housing, commuter students with disabilities have special facility requirements such as access to parking, ramps, and elevators. If the college has its own transportation system, it must also provide special lift-equipped vans or comparable services. In addition, physical accessibility must be afforded to buildings used by students, including classrooms, laboratories, and recreational facilities. With the ever-increasing demand for technology, computer and electronic equipment must also be adaptive to users with disabilities. Although postsecondary schools are required to follow federal mandates related to students with disabilities, they are not expected to lower or substantially alter their academic standards to accommodate these students, and they are not required to honor every accommodation request, especially if it poses undue financial or administrative hardship on the college or university (Brinkerhoff, Shaw, & McGuire, 1992; Vess, 2000).

A final area that warrants attention is graduation outcomes. It has been reported that graduates with disabilities require extra assistance with career planning and placement because they often have more difficulty finding employment than do graduates without disabilities. This is due in part to their lack of self-advocacy for obtaining accommodations and poor interviewing skills (Norton & Field, 1998).

RECOMMENDATIONS FOR SERVING DIVERSE STUDENTS

Among emerging best practices are early intervention to address academic problems, special needs programs, first-year college programs, tailored financial aid programs, and special mentoring and counseling programs. A promising practice is the involvement of an interdisciplinary team of college faculty, counselors, and administrators who work closely with at-risk students to identify needs and provide opportunities and connections to campus and community resources that will assist in the students' personal and professional development. This interdisciplinary approach can also serve as the foundation for the students' social and academic integration into the college setting.

This approach is supported by the work of Bean and Metzer (1985) and Tinto (1993), who have argued that academic and social integration into college life improves persistence. Also promising are professional development programs for faculty members and counselors to increase their skills in relating to the many adults who return to the education setting underprepared and with complex problems. The following are additional steps that community colleges can take to effectively serve diverse students:

- Review and revise policies, admission practices, and requirements.
- Upgrade curricula to meet changing demographic needs.
- Continuously offer training and retraining programs.
- Address changing demographics in mission statements and strategic plans.
- Equip faculty to accommodate various learning styles and alternative teaching methodologies.
- Provide social, learning, and cultural opportunities for students while placing more emphasis on life experience and learning portfolios than on standardized tests.
- Offer flexible scheduling and support services, such as weekend and evening classes, unconventional semesters, and flexible delivery formats through distance learning.
- Work with K–12 to improve the education pipeline, especially for underserved students, through dual enrollment and other collaborations between K–12 and postsecondary schools.

- Scrutinize the historical reliance on the deficit model, in which minority, low-income, nontraditional, and first-generation college students are characterized as having social and cultural deficiencies.
- Move toward the asset model, in which educators concentrate on skills, talents, and potential by developing strategies to complement student strengths and career goals.

REFERENCES

Adelman, C. (2005). *Moving into town—and moving on: The community college in the lives of traditional-age students.* Washington, DC: U.S. Department of Education.

Bean, J. P., & Metzer, B. S. (1985). A conceptual model of non-traditional undergraduate student attrition. *Review of Educational Research, 55*(4), 485–540.

Brinkerhoff, L. C., Shaw, S. F., & McGuire, J. M. (1992). Promoting access, accommodations and independence for college students with learning disabilities. *Journal of Learning Disabilities, 25*(7), 417–429.

Brint, S., & Karabel, J. (1989). *The diverted dream: Community colleges and the promise of educational opportunity in America, 1900–1985.* New York: Oxford University Press.

Chen, X., & Kaufman, P. (1997). *Risk and resilience: The effects of dropping out of school.* Paper presented at the meeting of the American Association of Educational Research, Chicago, IL. Available from the NCES Web site: http://nces.ed.gov/pubs

Cohen, A. M., & Brawer, F. B. (2003). *The American community college* (4th ed.). San Francisco: Jossey-Bass.

Coley, R. J. (2000). *The American community college turns 100: A look at its students, programs, and prospects* [Policy information report]. Princeton, NJ: Educational Testing Service. (ERIC # ED441553)

Culp, M., & Helfgot, S. (Eds.). (1998). *Life at the edge of the wave: Lessons from the community college.* Washington, DC: NASPA—Student Affairs Administrators in Higher Education. (ERIC # ED438888)

Eisen, M-J. (2005, Winter). Shifts in the landscape of learning: New challenges, new opportunities. *New Directions for Adult and Continuing Education, 2005*(108), 15–26.

Ender, K. L., Chand, S., & Thornton, J. S. (1996, Fall). Student affairs in the community college: Promoting student success and learning. *New Directions for Student Services, 1996*(75), 45–53.

Fry, R. (2002). *Hispanics in higher education: Many enroll, too few graduate.* Washington, DC: Pew Hispanic Center. Retrieved from the Pew Hispanic Center Web site: http://pewHispanic.org/files/reports/11.pdf. (ERIC # ED468848)

Gregg, N., Johnson, Y., & McKinley, C. (1996). Learning disabilities policy and legal issues: A consumer and practitioner user-friendly guide. In N. Gregg, C. Hoy, & A.F. Gay (Eds.), *Adults with learning disabilities: Theoretical and practical perspectives* (pp. 329–367). New York: Guilford Press.

Gregg, N., & Scott, S. S. (2000). Definition and documentation: Theory, measurement, and the courts. *Journal of Learning Disabilities, 33*(1), 5–13.

Grimes, S. K. (1997). Underprepared community college students: Characteristics, persistence, and academic success. *Community College Journal of Research & Practice, 21*(1), 47–57. Available from http://www.uah.edu/library. (Ebsco-Host # 9705086172)

Harvey, W. (2002). *Minorities in higher education: Nineteenth annual status report.* Washington, DC: American Council on Education.

Hawke, C. S. (2004, Spring). Accommodating students with disabilities. *New Directions for Community Colleges, 2004*(125), 17–27.

Kaufman, P., & Bradby, D. (1992). *Characteristics of at-risk students in NELS:88* (NCES 92-042). Washington, DC: U.S. Department of Education, National Center for Education Statistics.

Laanan, F. S. (2003). Older adults in community colleges: Choices, attitudes, and goals. *Educational Gerontology, 29*(9), 757–776.

Laden, B. V. (1998, April). *Celebratory socialization: Welcoming Hispanic students to college.* Paper presented at the meeting of the American Educational Research Association, San Diego, CA. (ERIC # ED 429523)

Laden, B. V. (2004). Hispanic-serving institutions: What are they? Where are they? *Community College Journal of Research and Practice, 28*(3), 181–198.

Latham, P. H. (2001). *Learning disabilities and the law: After high school: An overview for students.* Available from the Learning Disabilities Association of America Web site: http://www.ldaamerica.org

Lynch, R. T., & Gussel, L. (1996). Disclosure and self-advocacy regarding disability-related needs: Strategies to maximize integration in postsecondary education. *Journal of Counseling and Development, 74*(4), 352–357.

Merriam, S. B. (Ed.). (2001, Spring). The new update on adult learning theory. *New Directions for Adult and Continuing Education* (No. 89).

Nora, A. (2000). Reexamining the community college mission. *New expeditions: Charting the second century of community colleges.* Washington, DC: Association of Community College Trustees and American Association of Community Colleges. (ERIC # ED438871)

Norton, S., & Field, K. F. (1998). Career placement project: A career readiness program for community college students with disabilities. *Journal of Employment Counseling, 35*(1), 40–44. (ERIC # EJ567181)

Ortiz, A. M. (2004). Promoting the success of Hispanic students: A call to action. *New Directions for Student Services, 2004*(105), 89–97. (ERIC # EJ60814)

Pascarella, E., Wolniak, G., & Pierson, C. (2003). Explaining student growth in college when you don't think you are. *Journal of College Student Development, 44*(1), 122–126.

Prentice, M. (2002). Serving students with disabilities at the community college. *ERIC Digest.* (ERIC # ED467984)

Proctor, B. E. (2001). Social policy and its application to students with learning disabilities in U.S. institutes of higher education. *International Journal of Sociology and Social Policy, 21*(3), 38–59.

Rendon, L. I. (1992, Winter). From the barrio to the academy: Revelations of a Mexican American "scholarship girl." *New Directions for Community Colleges, 1992*(80), 55–64. (ERIC # EJ460062)

Romo, H. (1998). Latina high school leaving: Some practical solutions. *ERIC Digest.* (ERIC # ED423096)

Roueche, J. E., & Roueche, S. D. (1993). *Between a rock and a hard place: The at-risk student in the open-door college.* Washington, DC: American Association of Community Colleges. (ERIC # ED356015)

Ryan, E. F., (2003). Counseling non-traditional students at the community college. *ERIC Digest.* (ERIC # ED477913)

Seligman, M. E. P. (1975). *Helplessness: On depressions, development, and death.* San Francisco: W.H. Freeman.

Snyder, T. D., & Hoffman, C. M. (2002). *Digest of education statistics, 2001* (NCES 2002-130). Washington, DC: U.S. Department of Education, Institute of Education Sciences, National Center for Education Statistics.

Snyder, T. D., & Tan, A. G. (2005). *Digest of education statistics, 2004* (NCES 2006-005). Washington, DC: U.S. Department of Education, Institute of Education Sciences, National Center for Education Statistics.

Snyder, T. D., Tan, A. G., & Hoffman, C. M. (2006). *Digest of education statistics, 2005* (NCES 2006-030). Washington, DC: U.S. Department of Education, Institute of Education Sciences, National Center for Education Statistics.

Taylor, M. (2004). Widening participation into higher education for disabled students. *Journal of Education & Training, 46*(1), 40–48. Available from the Emerald Group Publishing Web site: www.emeraldinsight.com/0040-0912.htm

Terenzini, P., Cabrera, A., & Bernal, E. (2001). *Swimming against the tide: The poor in American higher education* (Research Report No. 2001-1). New York: The College Board.

Tinto, V. (1993). *Leaving college: Rethinking the causes and cures of student attrition.* Chicago: The University of Chicago Press.

U. S. Census Bureau. *U.S. census 2000: Demographic profiles* [Data file]. Washington, DC: Author.

Vess, S. (2000). Transition planning for postsecondary education. *NASP Communique, 28*(5), 18–19.

Wilds, D. J., & Wilson, R. (1998). *Minorities in higher education: Sixteenth annual status report.* Washington, DC: American Council on Education.

Yeh, T. L. (2002). Asian American college students who are educationally at risk. In M. K. McEwen, C. M. Kodama, A. N. Alvarez, S. Lee, & C. T. H. Liang (Eds.), *Working with Asian American college students* (pp. 61–72). San Francisco: Jossey-Bass.

Zwerling, L. S. (Ed.). (1986). The community college and its critics. *New Directions for Community Colleges, 1986*(54), 127.

Chapter 3

Advice for Leaders Advancing the Open-Door Philosophy

Curtis L. Ivery

As a community college leader, I advocate and advance the defining characteristic of the community college: the open door to educational opportunity and success. The open door represents a set of beliefs that unite community college professionals at the local, state, and national levels. I believe that talent and ambition are widely distributed in our society; that everyone should have the opportunity to achieve their goals through education; and that a supportive, nurturing learning environment will empower students to reach their potential. In doing so, these students will contribute not only to their own betterment but also to that of their families, neighborhoods, and communities.

Not since the 1960s have community colleges experienced such dramatically changing conditions. We are challenged to implement transformational rather than incremental change in order to continue to be "democracy's colleges." Just as earlier community college leaders projected a compelling vision of the open-door college that inspired us to action, our generation of leaders must articulate a vision that will unite community college practitioners in a common cause: We must recreate the foundation of the community college and embrace a new definition of the open door.

Andy Grove (1996), founder of Intel, described what he called "strategic inflection points"—times at which an organization must make massive changes in response to dramatically changed conditions in order to remain competitive. At such a point, the organization must either reinvent itself or become irrelevant to the changing needs of those to be served. Community colleges are now facing a strategic inflection point. The old model of the open door, which focused on making higher education accessible to those who would otherwise be denied, is moving toward a new, more comprehensive model. This new model continues to embrace student access, but it also emphasizes student success, campuswide inclusiveness, and community engagement. Community colleges must reinvent themselves in response to external pressures such as expanding diversity, the achievement gap between minority and majority groups, racial resegregation in urban areas, economic uncertainty, failing public schools, and the global economy.

Just as community college leaders of the 1960s and 1970s changed U.S. higher education by granting greater access to higher education, leaders today can bring the open door inside the college to focus on student success and college inclusiveness and reach out once again to reinvent community engagement. We need not wait for the future to shape us; we can shape the future. The potential for community college leaders, faculty members, staff members, and community supporters to create the best future for our students, communities, and colleges is unlimited. However, the transformation will require addressing entrenched practices, stereotypical behaviors, anti-change attitudes, and limited resources. To overcome these roadblocks, the successful community college leader must believe passionately in the mission and be devoted to the underlying open-door philosophy.

DIRECTIVES FOR OPEN-DOOR ADVOCATES

1. Reinforce the Community College Mission

As an open-door advocate, I believe that the mission of the community college is to empower individuals, businesses, and communities to achieve their goals through excellent and accessible educational programs and services. The mission statement expresses why the college exists by articulating its social role. The various functions of the college (university transfer, general education, career education, student services, developmental education, workforce development, and continuing education) are the means by which the mission is carried out. These functions are what the college does to achieve its mission.

Critics of the community college who argue for the primacy of university transfer programs, career education, or degree-granting programs do not fully understand the mission of the open-door community college (e.g., some argue that degree completion should be the core mission). These critics typically seek a targeted mission, arguing that community colleges cannot be all things to all people. They object to expansion into areas such as developmental education, workforce development, continuing education, and community engagement. They do not understand that the uniqueness of the open-door community college lies in its responsiveness, nimbleness, and relevance to local conditions and trends. The programmatic emphasis required to achieve the mission is a matter for the local leaders to decide. Of course, limited resources necessitate making hard choices, but these choices are best made by local leaders who understand the local realities. Maintaining the open door means creating keys to education opportunity within the communities being served, not limiting the range of services because of an arbitrary hierarchy imposed by external forces.

2. Know the Specific Needs of the Community You Serve

I encourage senior community college leaders to take the balcony view as they consider strategies that will best serve an increasingly diverse range of constituencies. The senior leadership team of a community college must consider the big picture. The big picture certainly includes international, national, and state considerations, and local community college leaders should be involved in and influenced by these considerations.

However, those of us at local colleges bring a grassroots, bottom-up perspective to strategy development. The senior leaders can guide the transformation of the open door model by positioning themselves in the middle of the two-way flow of messages between the college and community constituencies about changing education needs. If the senior leadership team is aware of only a portion of the information and static flowing between the college and community about needs, opinions, and complaints, the team will inevitably make some decisions that are unresponsive to emerging education needs. The mandate to the senior team should be to know more than anyone else knows about the demographic, economic, educational, and cultural dimensions of the community.

3. Advocate for Underserved and Underprepared Groups

The community college leader must be an advocate for keeping the door of educational opportunity open for underserved and underprepared groups in the communities served, especially for minority, low-income, and unemployed groups that have little capacity to advocate for themselves. This advocacy can take place in a number of forums at the local, state, and national levels. As fierce advocates for the open door, we can educate leaders in business, government, labor, education, and religious and nonprofit organizations about the importance of empowering underserved and underprepared groups to use education as the pathway to the economic mainstream. Furthermore, we can gain the support and engagement of community leaders in programs that will benefit not only our students and their families, but also the economic health of the community. We can raise private funds through the college's foundation to provide scholarships for low-income people. Internally, the senior leaders of the college can be the advocates for innovations in admissions, financial aid, developmental education, supplemental instruction, diversity and multicultural programs, student retention efforts, and other innovations that make the college a more welcoming and equitable place for those who might otherwise be excluded.

Wayne County Community College District (WCCCD) in Detroit is a participant in the Achieving the Dream initiative, a national program that focuses on increasing the academic attainment of minority and low-income students as well as those who experience barriers to career and academic success due to limited literacy and job skills and other personal and family factors. Through this initiative, the community colleges involved seek to minimize, or even eliminate, the achievement gap between the targeted students and the general student population. The objective is to create systemic, long-lasting interventions that change the core policies, programs, and practices of community colleges.

At WCCCD, research has led to addressing improvements in student advising and course placement processes, developmental education, student retention, and institutional research capacity. Starting with baseline data on the academic achievement of the targeted student cohort, WCCCD is working to increase the academic performance of these students by piloting interventions, assessing the impact on student achievement, and scaling the most effective interventions to the five campuses in service to all students. As all Achieving the Dream colleges engage in similar continuous improvement efforts, it is hoped that the most effective practices can be scaled to community colleges across the country.

4. Base Decisions on Real Data

Community college professionals understand and support the movement toward increased accountability for results that justify the public's financial investment in higher education. Agencies of the federal government, accrediting bodies, and business organizations all are demanding greater results for their money. Many issues have sparked this demand for greater "bang for the buck," a primary one being that minority and other underserved and underprepared groups must be an integral part of a globally competitive U.S. workforce. Yet, in spite of substantial investment in education, a low percentage of these groups earn the high school and college credentials needed for success in the emerging knowledge economy.

The accountability movement can be a boon to the evolution of the community college's open door because it requires a focus on the success of all students, regardless of their backgrounds, and thus it gives life and shape to the student success dimension of the new open-door model. To measure accountability, questions must be asked about the percentage of students who successfully pass developmental education courses, move successfully from developmental education to college-level courses, complete college-level courses with a *C* or better, and complete certificate and degree programs. Information obtained from assessing student learning outcomes and from evaluating the performance of noninstructional college units against a set of excellence indicators becomes the evidence that guides improvement decisions and budget allocations.

5. Align Strategy With the Ability to Execute It

Bossidy and Charan (2002) warned that no worthwhile strategy can be successful without considering the organization's ability to execute it. In these turbulent times, it is especially difficult to execute major institutional change in the face of an increasingly diverse student body with changing education needs, businesses experiencing economic challenges, and communities adapting to changing realities. Because of these challenging conditions, community college leaders are more likely to fail in executing an institutional strategy than in formulating and articulating the strategy. To build the capacity to execute the strategy of reinventing the open door, community college leaders must align all key internal processes to the strategy—including policy development, strategic and annual planning, leadership development, faculty and staff professional development, curriculum development, resource development and allocation, and student services development—and strengthening and modifying these processes as needed.

Aligning Strategy With the Ability to Execute It at WCCCD

In 2002, WCCCD embarked on the Pathways to the Future initiative to guide and execute the districtwide transformation of programs, services, facilities, structures, and systems. This mission-driven initiative embraces student access, student success, campuswide inclusiveness, and community engagement. This type of transformation requires intense attention to executing the strategy within the core dimensions of the college, such as

- Fully implementing mission-driven indicators of effectiveness.
- Increasing the pace of curriculum development.
- Building a culture of evidence that includes strengthening the assessment of student learning outcomes and using assessment data to improve learning, teaching, and institutional practices.
- Managing the changing role of the faculty in assessing student learning outcomes.
- Transforming student support services.
- Engaging every administrative service in the support of student learning.
- Infusing unique applications of the open-door mission in distance education and other technology-assisted learning.
- Promoting more entrepreneurial approaches to engagement in community problem solving.

SHAPING THE FUNDAMENTALS OF A NEW OPEN-DOOR MODEL AT WCCCD

WCCCD is one of the nation's largest metropolitan multicampus community college districts, serving 32 communities and townships, including the city of Detroit, which poses many challenges. Detroit is the most segregated city in the nation; it has one of the highest poverty and crime rates; its public schools have one of the highest dropout rates in the nation; and in Detroit and many other sections of Wayne County, the adult illiteracy rate is very high compared with other areas of Michigan.

In this turbulent urban and metropolitan setting, WCCCD seeks to be an oasis of hope, opportunity, and potential by serving people of all kinds—poor and rich, young and old, skilled and unskilled, straight and gay—and from many different racial, ethnic, and national backgrounds. The student body mirrors that which is emerging in many community colleges across the United States. WCCCD's current experience might serve as a prototype of what many other community colleges will experience in the coming years. To respond to its expanding diversity, WCCCD has worked since 2002 to transform its programs, services, facilities, structures, and processes. To launch this transformation, WCCCD has updated its foundational documents (mission, values, function, and vision statements) and its strategic goals as follows.

Mission

"WCCCD's mission is to empower individuals, businesses and communities to achieve their goals through excellent and accessible services, culturally diverse experiences, and globally competitive higher education and career advancement programs" (WCCCD, 2009). The purpose of updating the mission statement, approved by the board of trustees in 2007, was to place increased emphasis on both accessibility and excellence and to express a commitment to cultural diversity and empowering students to succeed in a global community.

Values

The 2007 update of WCCCD's statement of values included—in addition to statements on supporting excellence in teaching and learning, serving the common good, being accountable, and operating with integrity—a statement on honoring diversity: "We honor the worth of individuals of all racial, gender, ethnic, and national origins, and we value persons of all socioeconomic, educational, and experiential backgrounds. We value our role as 'democracy's college' providing an open door of education opportunity to all who can benefit from our services. We help our students to live responsibly in a global society by nurturing in them an increased appreciation and understanding of diverse cultures and ideas" (WCCCD, 2008).

Vision 2011

In 2007, WCCCD updated its vision statement to include this sentence: "WCCCD will focus on continuous self-evaluation and self-improvement; preparation of a highly skilled workforce in support of the Wayne County economy; student academic and career success; and leadership in strengthening the open-door philosophy of educational opportunity" (WCCCD, 2009).

Strategic Goals and Objectives

The first of seven strategic goals for 2009–2014 is advancement of the open door "by focusing on student access, diversity, equity, multicultural experiences, campus inclusiveness, and community engagement" (WCCCD, 2008). Objectives of this goal are as follows:

- The student success interventions planned as part of WCCCD's partnership with the national Achieving the Dream initiative: student advisement, developmental education, student retention, and institutional research capacity.
- Continuation of WCCCD's national leadership role in promoting the reinvention of the community college's open door.
- The integration of diversity, equity, multicultural, campus inclusiveness, and community engagement efforts into one unified initiative.
- The enhancement and redesign of student services with an emphasis on a customer-service culture, high school partnerships, student recruitment, student engagement, financial aid, technology-assisted student support services, and outreach to diverse community groups.

Other strategic goals are expansion of community engagement, advancement of instructional innovation, strengthening of processes to support effective student learning, development of institutional resources, enhancement of districtwide continuous self-evaluation and self-improvement, and advancement of operational and management excellence.

REFERENCES

Bossidy, L., & Charan, R. (2002) *Execution: The discipline of getting things done.* New York: Crown Business.

Grove, A. S. (1996). *Only the paranoid survive: How to identify and exoploit the crisis points that challenge very business.* New York, NY: Doubleday Business.

Wayne County Community College District. (2008). *Wayne County Community College District 2009–2014 strategic plan: Leading WCCCD to enduring excel-*

lence through a focus on student success and college-wide effectiveness. Detroit, MI: Wayne County Community College, Office of the Chancellor. Retrieved from http://www.wcccd.edu/about/pdfs/WCCCD-StrategicPlan.pdf

Wayne County Community College District. (2009). *Mission statement.* Retrieved from http://www.wcccd.edu/about/mission.htm

Chapter 4

Higher Education Access for Underprepared Students

John Bolden

Community colleges are transforming the definition and practice of access to higher education and to the economic mainstream, particularly for those who are underprepared for these life-changing opportunities. The traditional model for access was developed during the social revolution of the 1960s when minorities and other groups demanded an end to historic exclusion from higher education. Often called open admissions, the model was activated when the student applied for admission, and its primary mechanisms to achieve readiness for college-level work included internal services such as admissions testing, orientation, course placement, financial aid, tutorial services, and developmental education programs.

Although this traditional access model has been strikingly effective in increasing enrollment of previously disenfranchised groups, many still find access to college-level study unattainable because of the lack of preparedness. The reality is that too many high school graduates today do not have the skills to do college-level work. Racial and ethnic minorities are the most poorly served by public education, including the fast-growing Hispanic population, which has the lowest rate of education attainment.

A report by the National Center for Public Policy and Higher Education (2005) indicated that the United States lags behind other countries in attainment of college degrees among the young workforce. The report highlighted the facts that the U.S. workforce is becoming more diverse and that the racial and ethnic groups that are the least educated are the fastest growing. The impact of these twin facts is that if current population trends continue and states do not improve education for all racial and ethnic groups, the skills of the workforce and incomes of U.S. residents are projected to decline over the next two decades. Because those who are underprepared are likely to become an economic liability when they could be contributing members of the highly skilled workforce needed to compete in a global economy, it is clear that a national education and economic disaster is in the making. For this reason, community colleges are partnering with other leaders to reinvent the model for access to higher education.

NEW LEVELS OF CONNECTION WITH SCHOOLS AND COMMUNITY AGENCIES

During most of their history, community colleges have been only marginally involved in the life events of prospective students prior to admission. Although there was a level of cooperation among the typical community college, local high schools, and other agencies providing youth and adult education services, each operated largely in its own silo with its own standards, policies, programs, and structures. This disconnect between the vertical levels of education and the horizontal sectors of community-based adult education and community services has resulted in practices that are confusing to and dysfunctional for students. Students have been basically on their own to negotiate the maze between the various institutions and even the processes within them.

The emerging new model for access breaks down the policy, programmatic, and procedural walls that separate the institutions. It places more responsibility on leaders at all levels to empower students to be fully ready for the collegiate experience. Community colleges are crossing the borders that existed between them and the feeder institutions by becoming directly involved in shaping the ways in which these institutions prepare students to meet the standards for enrollment in college.

This border-crossing model can involve partnerships with many community agencies, but it primarily affects secondary and adult education programs in the college's service area. The emerging access model continues to embrace traditional elements within the college itself, such as orientation programs, admissions testing, financial aid, course placement, tutorial services, and developmental education, while adding community-based dimensions that feature partnerships with public schools and other community organizations involved in youth and adult education.

PREPAREDNESS THROUGH COMMUNITY COLLEGE–SECONDARY SCHOOL PARTNERSHIPS

In a 2006 joint statement, the American Council on Education (ACE) and five other higher education organizations, including AACC, referred to the shortcomings of secondary schools in preparing students for higher education as a growing crisis especially affecting low-income students: "As a nation, we are disenfranchising many in our society by not adequately educating them in our elementary and secondary schools" (ACE et al., 2006). In response, community colleges are reinventing their connections with secondary schools with a focus on joint processes that increase the number of secondary students who are prepared for college and career pathways.

The new access model must address factors that cause the lack of academic preparedness and college participation among at-risk high school students. These factors include a lack of awareness and understanding of college costs and financial aid by those who might think that college is financially unattainable; a lack of adequately trained student advisers in schools; limited knowledge of college-entry requirements; the invisible barrier of a high school's low academic expectations; and perceptions of racial hostility and lack of merit (McDonough, 2004). Added to this list are the student's lack of knowledge of career opportunities and pathways from high school to a career; limited English proficiency; lack of conditioning to be involved in rigorous learning activities; confusion based on conflicting information from teachers, counselors, and administrators about what must be learned and what is needed to enter college; and lack of clear career, academic, and other life goals and structured ways to achieve them.

Many community colleges are cooperating with area high schools to bring about holistic solutions that address these at-risk factors. For example, Capital Community College in Connecticut begins the outreach to area schools starting with fifth graders who are invited to the college to experience classes and tour the campus. Middle school children participate in activities such as an early college awareness day, a YMCA minority achievers' program, and a science academy. High school students are offered a number of opportunities to enter programs that bridge between high school and college, including college readiness and preprofessional career preparation. Aims Community College in Colorado offers the Weld County High School Diploma Program, which enables would-be dropouts and out-of-school adults to graduate from high school. Entering students take the WorkKeys tests in applied math, applied technology, locating information, listening, observation, reading for information, teamwork, and writing. Students must achieve a required standard in each area to graduate, and they must defend their portfolios before a committee of community representatives (ACT, Inc., 2009).

Most community colleges participate in federal programs such as TRIO, which is designed to provide college preparation services to low-income and first-generation college students. Talent Search and Upward Bound are related examples of federal efforts to use community colleges to sponsor intervention strategies that empower students to graduate from high school and pursue a college program. Gaining Early Awareness and Readiness for Undergraduate Programs (GEAR UP) is another federal program designed to bring together colleges, secondary schools, and other community agencies to work in a systemic way with economically disadvantaged youth and their families to prepare them for college and career progression. Portland Community College in Oregon and Tri-County Technical College in South Carolina provide gateway programs designed to enable at-risk high school students and recent dropouts to earn their diplomas while simultaneously working toward a college certificate or degree.

Additional examples of best practices that address the underpreparation of secondary school students include Bridges to Opportunity for Underprepared Adults. Funded by the Ford Foundation, Bridges is "a multi-year effort designed to bring about changes in state policy that improve education and employment outcomes for educationally and economically disadvantaged adults" (Ford Foundation, 2008). To that end, it provides grants and assistance to community colleges in six states: Colorado, Kentucky, Louisiana, New Mexico, Ohio, and Washington.

Another best practice is the Bridge Partnership of the National Alliance of Community and Technical Colleges (NACTC). The program promotes and supports the development of community college–high school partnerships with the following goals:

- To increase the number of high school students, especially minorities, who aspire to a college education.
- To decrease the level of deficiency of students who complete high school unprepared to begin standard college courses.
- To encourage community colleges to work closely with feeder high schools to offer their college placement examinations to high school students as early as the second half of the sophomore year.
- To inform high school students and their parents or guardians of the difference between high school graduation requirements and requirements to enroll in college credit courses (NACTC, 2009).

Bridge partnerships shift the definition of high school–to–college transition to a broader and more in-depth definition that encompasses college preparation activities starting in the 10th grade. The college and school work together to agree on the competencies students develop in high school in order for them to be successful in standard college classes and to then work to improve curricular coordination. The college placement examination is given to students as early as 10th grade, and the high school agrees to use the examination results to plan the remainder of the student's secondary program. Students who meet the competencies criteria receive a certificate for admission to the community college without further admissions testing.

Bridge partnerships have been formed in the Houston-area Lone Star College System, formerly known as the North Harris Montgomery Community College District. With nearly 59,000 credit students now attending its five separate community colleges, the system is one of about 50 that have formed bridge partnerships with local high schools since the program's inception 8 years ago, according to NACTC Executive Director Robert McCabe. At Lone Star and elsewhere, the partnership aims to reduce the number of college freshmen needing remedial courses in reading, writing, and math; to assist students in making a successful transition from high school to college; and to increase the number of students who achieve their education goals. In its first partnership year (2004–2005), Lone Star enrolled more than 500 students from seven high schools. Tenth graders took college placement exams, and those who tested below college-ready were provided with extensive academic advisement and guided to take appropriate high school courses to become college-ready. As a result, the high school–college curricular alignment was improved, and better data were obtained on the correlation between high school preparation and college success. The high school students and their parents became more aware of the college's educational resources and the advantages of beginning college at a community college. As a result, the high schools introduced new courses, changed student advising policies, and encouraged students to enroll in dual high school–college credit courses.

To accelerate its own strategy to assist high school students in becoming better prepared for college, Wayne County Community College District (WCCCD), in partnership with the Detroit public schools, applied to a foundation for support of an intervention program that introduced students to the college environment in the 9th grade. From earlier experiences with high school students through dual and concurrent enrollment and an analysis of their matriculation patterns, WCCCD knew that it was essential to establish a clear path for these students to succeed in college. The college and school system identified major barriers to enrollment and academic performance in higher education and requested funds from the foundation to address those barriers in transportation, textbooks, study and learning strategies, career information, self-confidence, and parental and school support. In keeping with the program design of successful transition, college and school officials established a number of intervals for participation of parents as well as the school system's teachers and counselors.

WCCCD is participating in another program with the Detroit Public Schools and a major employer, the Detroit Medical Center. This program is designed to be housed on a WCCCD campus and extend to the first year of college in order to allow students to achieve skills in health-science occupations that will prepare them for immediate employment at one of the medical facilities of the Detroit Medical Center or to transfer to a 4-year college or university. Staff from Detroit Public Schools and WCCCD have worked together to develop the appropriate curriculum strands that will integrate job shadowing, apprenticeships, and internships with the academic curriculum. The project began with its first ninth graders this fall, and it will expose them to actual careers through a summer program at the hospital at the end of their ninth and tenth grades.

Another initiative to improve services to underprepared youth and adults is the College and Career Transitions Initiative (CCTI), administered by the League for Innovation in the Community College and funded by the U.S. Department of Education's Office of Vocational and Adult Education. This project focuses on the alignment of high school, community college, and university career education programs in industry-monitored, high-demand career fields. CCTI has created site partnerships with selected community colleges in the career fields of education and training; health science; information technology; law, public safety, and security; and science, technology, engineering, and mathematics. Through partnerships with local high schools, these community college site partners worked to improve joint public school–community college transitional initiatives such as dual enrollment, middle college, tech prep, and advanced placement. In addition, the CCTI Network, which is open to all community colleges, is designed to help community colleges share information on efforts to improve the readiness of high school students and adults to choose and prepare for a career (see, e.g., Warford, 2006).

Dual high school and community college enrollment, also sometimes called concurrent enrollment or dual-credit enrollment, is commonly used to prepare students for college. Juniors and seniors take college-level classes from the local community college, earning dual credit that counts concurrently toward their high school diploma and a college certificate or associate degree. Nearly every state allows dual enrollment, and the majority of public schools and community colleges cooperate in offering it. However, the means of financing the program varies from state to state. Some community colleges blend the dual-enrollment students into regular college classes, whereas others might provide separate class sections just for them. Dual-enrollment courses can be taught on the college campus, at a high school, or online. Although it is generally felt that dual-enrollment programs are designed for academically talented and self-motivated high school students, there are also opportunities for less academically able and unmotivated students to take college-level occupational courses as a means of reviving their enthusiasm for learning and introducing them to the benefits of the college experience.

A final example of emerging best practices that create a bridge between high school and college for underprepared students is the charter school or early college, also sometimes called the middle college. The Bill and Melinda Gates Foundation promotes early college programs that permit high school students to complete their diplomas and move toward associate degrees. One of the pioneers in middle colleges is the program at LaGuardia Community College in New York. LaGuardia Community College sponsors a middle college high school on its campus for students who are at risk of dropping out. It has become a national model as a means of intervention to reverse the dropout rate. Another example is the Washtenaw Technical Middle College (WTMC) at Washtenaw Community College (Michigan). Operating as a public school under state charter school provisions, WTMC is housed on the Washtenaw Community College campus and benefits from access to the campus resources including the extensive technical education offerings. WTMC students attend required high school completion classes as a separate high school group, but they mix with regular college students to take college-level technical courses.

BRIDGING BETWEEN ADULT EDUCATION AND COMMUNITY COLLEGE PROGRAMS

The Council for Advancement of Adult Literacy (CAAL) estimated that there are 30–50 million adults with low basic skills or inadequate language proficiency. Of this number, CAAL estimates that about 3 million enroll in adult education programs each year (Spangenberg, 2005). Nevertheless, a report by the U.S. Secretary of Education's Commission on the Future of Higher Education called attention to the fact that there is little national discussion about adult learners in higher education. The report indicates that, although adult learners are everywhere, they remain invisible—hidden in plain sight. They are curiously absent from the dialogue concerning the purpose and mission of higher education. Because community colleges are primary pathways to college and career success for low-skilled adults, it is incumbent on community college leaders to serve as advocates for this important constituency.

Adult education is more important than ever, with employment in the global economy requiring not only high school but also college credits or college credentials. Michigan, like most other states, feels the impact of this force as more technician jobs are being outsourced and low-skill, low-wage jobs are being left for the undereducated. These citizens remain on the fringes of society, moving from one unskilled job to another and in and out of training programs.

Adult education students are also challenged by their marginality to education. For many, their experiences with secondary education were traumatic. They dropped out of high school for reasons ranging from an ill parent to a coach who embarrassed them in front of their peers or gang members who attempted to recruit them.

One half of community colleges provide adult education services, and a third of all adult students attend community colleges. These colleges serve a disproportionate share of the economically disadvantaged, racial minorities, and immigrants compared with other colleges and universities (Spangenberg, 2005). In the fall of 2002, adults between the ages of 25 and 64 represented 35% of full-time-equivalent enrollments in community colleges, compared with only 15% in 4-year public colleges and universities. More than two thirds of those adult students at community colleges were classified as low-income (Prince & Jenkins, 2005).

BUILDING THE STEPS TO SUCCESS

Although some adult students will be prepared for college, most first need to take adult education or developmental education courses to upgrade their reading, writing, math, and study skills. A highly motivated person with low literacy and computational skills can be successful in developmental education, but most will benefit from starting at the adult education level. Therefore, the community college must build the steps that enable adults to traverse this ladder of skill development progress: adult education, developmental education, and college-level courses and programs.

1. Adult Education

CAAL defines adult basic education as improving reading, writing, and math for adults who are functioning below the ninth-grade level. Adult secondary education focuses on upgrading knowledge and skills to the high school equivalency level and preparing adults to take high school equivalency tests such as the General Educational Development (GED) test. English as a second language (ESL) programs provide instruction at the precollegiate level (Spangenberg, 2005).

At WCCCD, an emerging best practice is the blending of traditional adult education with basic job-skills development. The district offers more than 80 occupational programs. Students who qualify are eligible for financial aid to support their enrollment in career and technical programs while completing their GEDs. This serves as a powerful motivator for those who are older and need to become employable as quickly as possible. Also effective are short-term programs that serve as career ladders, such as one-year surgical technician or emergency medical technician courses. After students complete these courses and pass their GED tests, they can enter employment and continue with evening or part-time classes to earn an associate degree.

2. Developmental Education

For adults who can function at the ninth-grade level or higher in reading, writing, and math, developmental education (sometimes called remedial education) will help close the gap between their current skills and the level needed to succeed in regular college courses and programs. In some cases, adults can take developmental education courses in conjunction with selected collegiate courses; in other cases, students must complete the developmental course sequences before enrolling in college-level courses.

3. College-Level Courses and Programs

Research indicates that students who complete the developmental education course sequence leading to a certificate or associate degree program are as likely to complete the certificate or degree as are students who did not require developmental education. In addition, low-skilled adults who complete a developmental education sequence and receive financial aid are two to three times as likely to earn a certificate or associate degree as are those who did not receive these supportive services. Attending college for at least one year and earning a credential provided the basis for a substantial boost in earnings for adults (Prince & Jenkins, 2005).

ACCESS: A MATTER OF PERCEPTION

As community colleges consider strategies for improving adult education, the following perceptions and concerns of low-skilled adult learners should be taken into account:

- Many need to work, and they have difficulty balancing the demands of work and schooling.
- Many do not clearly see the connection between a community college education and their career progression.
- Many do not know how to gain access to supportive services such as tutoring, financial aid, and career counseling.
- Many do not receive support from their family and friends, including for child care, transportation, and finances.
- Many lack proficiency in English and mathematics, and they may be fearful of these gatekeeper courses that stand between them and success.
- Many lack clear learning and career goals.
- Many have difficulty persisting in a program that may cover several semesters.
- Many see a college certificate as beyond their reach.
- Many perceive a lack of connection and continuity between various programs such as basic adult education, GED, and the college's developmental education program.

⌁⌁⌁

Community colleges are ensuring access to higher education in response to the barriers to success faced by low-skilled and underprepared youth and adults. They are crossing borders to create new action-oriented partnerships with secondary schools and other community, state, and national organizations. These partnerships are producing systemic change at both the school and college levels in terms of governing policies, curricula, teaching practices, student support services, and instructor and staff professional development. As well, community colleges are inventing customized approaches to serving the low-skilled and underprepared students who enroll in adult education and developmental education programs. These approaches include

- Formation of student support groups.
- Modularization of courses to minimize course load.
- Child-care services.
- Financial aid counseling.
- Coordination of instruction with work schedules.
- Paid release-time arrangements with employers.
- Counseling to establish short- and long-range goals.

- Case management to monitor progress toward individual goals.
- Open entry–open exit arrangements.
- Professional development programs for instructors.
- Competency-based instruction.
- Assessment tools to enable instructors to identify appropriate interventions in problem areas.

As demonstrated by these promising innovations, community college leaders are working with their school and community partners to reinvent the ways in which at-risk students make the transition from secondary school and adult education programs to community college courses and programs. In doing so, they are providing life-changing opportunities to those who might otherwise continue to exist in the economic underclass.

REFERENCES

ACT, Inc. (2009, July). *Case study: WorkKeys helps at-risk high school students earn a diploma and prepare for a brighter future.* Retrieved from http://www.act.org/workkeys/case/aims.html

American Council on Education, American Association of State Colleges and Universities, American Association of Community Colleges, Association of American Universities, National Association of Independent Colleges and Universities, and National Association of State Universities and Land-Grant Colleges. (2006, September 21). *Addressing the challenges facing American undergraduate education. A letter to our nembers: Next steps* [Joint statement]. Available on the American Council of Education Web site: http://www.acenet.edu

Ford Foundation. (2008). *Bridges to opportunity for underprepared adults: A state policy guide for community college leaders.* Retrieved from http://www.fordfound.org/pdfs/impact/Bridges_to_Opportunity_for_Underprepared_Adults.pdf

McDonough, P. M. (2004) *The school-to-college transition: Challenges and prospects.* Washington, DC: American Council on Education, Center for Policy Study. Retrieved from http://www.acenet.edu/bookstore/pdf/2004_IPtransitions.pdf

National Alliance of Community and Technical Colleges. (2009). *The Bridge Partnership: Strengthening the path from 10th grade to college success.* Retrieved from http://nactc.org/#tab=7

National Center for Public Policy and Higher Education. (2005, November). *Income of U.S. workforce projected to decline if education doesn't improve* [Policy alert]. San Jose, CA: Retrieved from http://www.highereducation.org/reports/pa_decline/pa_decline.pdf

Prince, D., & Jenkins, D. (2005). *Building pathways to success for low-skill adult stu-*

dents: Lessons for community college policy and practice from a longitudinal tracking study.* New York: Columbia University, Community College Research Center, Teachers College. Retrieved from http://ccrc.tc.columbia.edu/Publication.asp?UID=204

Spangenberg, G. (Ed.). (2005, February). *To ensure America's future: Building a national opportunity system for adults: Strengthening links between adult education and community colleges.* New York: Council for Advancement of Adult Literacy. Retrieved from http://www.caalusa.org/ensureamericasfuture.pdf

Warford, L. J. (Ed.). (2006). *Pathways to student success: Case studies from the college and career transitions initiative.* Phoenix, AZ: League for Innovation in the Community College. Retrieved from http://www.league.org/projects/ccti/files/CCTI_Pathway_Book.pdf

Chapter 5

Student Success in the New Open-Door Community College

Gunder Myran

Most community college professionals are painfully aware that access to higher education is not enough. Community college leaders are bombarded with demands from government, business leaders, and accreditation agencies for evidence of student achievement and demonstration of return on investment, and an increasingly diverse student body seeks to achieve academic and career success. The student success element of the open-door model involves identifying learning goals; assessing learning outcomes; continuously improving teaching, courses, programs, and the college as a whole, based on the evidence of student achievement; and monitoring the improvements to determine whether they increase student achievement.

It is popular today to speak of the community college as a learning college. Instead of referring to the schools as teaching institutions, we now refer to them as learning-centered or learner-centered institutions; the emphasis has shifted from teaching and instructors to learning and students. Curricula design, teaching methods, and other institutional practices are now judged by the degree to which students have achieved the intended outcomes of the course or program and by the success of graduates in the workplace or the university to which they transferred. Not only are instructors responsible for learning outcomes, so are all members of the staff, including the president. The collegewide commitment to student learning and success is illustrated by a program at Coastline Community College (California) as described by its president, Ding-Jo H. Currie: "Last year at Coastline, we launched 'Power of One.'

Each of us, regardless of our role as administrator, instructor, or support staff, possesses the power to transform a student's life" (Currie, 2007).

RECOGNIZING BARRIERS TO SUCCESS FOR A DIVERSE STUDENT BODY

Although most community college professionals know that access is not enough, they also know how difficult it is to create a learning college that is centered on student retention and achievement. It has been said that, unlike elite universities, community colleges do not select winners, they create them. Community college students are much more likely than those at 4-year colleges and universities to have risk factors as they seek to earn a college certificate or degree: lack of preparation for college, delayed entry to college after high school, first-generation college attendance, part-time college attendance, working full time while attending college, dependents at home, and single parenthood. Data from the U.S. Department of Education, as analyzed by the Community College Research Center (cited in Achieving the Dream, 2007) confirm the challenge that community colleges face in empowering students to overcome barriers to success and become productive members of society:

- Only 45% of community college students who seek an associate or higher degree or who transfer to a 4-year college or university complete their objective within 6 years.
- 29% of community college students have a household income of less than $20,000.
- 35% of community college students are parents or have other dependents. (17% are single parents.)
- 41% of community college students are the first from their family to attend college.
- 69% of community college students attend college part time.
- 41% of community college students have full-time jobs in addition to taking classes.

Community college students face both personal and institutional barriers to career and academic success. In addition to the items listed above, they might lack some of the personal conditions that contribute to success, such as dependable child care, employer flexibility, a safety net of public assistance, personal counseling, and support from family and friends. Students might also face barriers created by the community college itself. Frequent complaints, especially from minority and low-income students, include an unwelcoming environment, language barriers, instructors not experienced in dealing with diverse students, racial stereotyping, the lack of adequate and accessible financial aid, and difficulty in gaining needed information.

THE UPHILL PATH TO A COLLEGE CULTURE OF LEARNING AND SUCCESS

Community college leaders face a rocky, uphill path as they work to reinvent the student success element of the open-door model. According to the 2007 Community College Survey of Student Engagement (CCSSE), personal factors have more effect on the level of student achievement than do institutional support factors. That is, a student's financial and family circumstances are likely to have more effect than do the college's developmental education and tutorial programs and other support services. This is the challenge that community leaders face: to increase the positive effect of institutional policies and practices on student achievement. Ultimately, community college leaders must create a culture of learning and success in which all institutional programs, services, structures, and processes are oriented toward, and judged by their effect on, learning.

Although substantial success can be noted, community colleges are in the early stages of creating a true culture of learning and success. In such a culture, improvement and resource allocation decisions at the course, program, and institutional levels are based on student achievement. Assessment of effectiveness based on student satisfaction and success becomes a way of life. As they move toward a culture of learning and success, many colleges struggle with the collection and interpretation of student performance data. Instructors and staff are not accustomed to using performance data as a basis for decisions and actions in the classroom or in the executive office. When leaders seek to identify in measurable terms the learning outcomes for courses and programs and when they seek to establish the means of assessing learning outcomes, they may be seen as invading the territory of instructors.

Although resistance from instructors is a factor in the slow pace of transition from a teaching to a learning college, the lack of involvement and commitment by administrators is also a factor. In some colleges, there is little evidence that planning priorities and budget allocations reflect a commitment to the learning college. In addition, instructors and administrators often lack the capacity and expertise to articulate student learning goals, create learning-outcome assessment tools, and design interventions that work. These are some of the hurdles that community college leaders must overcome as they seek to fulfill the promise of the learning college.

INDICATORS OF SUCCESS

What constitutes student success in the community college? What are the indicators that help community college leaders determine whether students are successful? The Achieving the Dream: Community Colleges Count initiative has the goal of determining ways in which community colleges can increase student achievement, with a focus on minority and low-income students. Approximately 86 community colleges are currently involved in this national initiative. The Achieving the Dream initiative has identified some practical, straightforward indicators of student achievement that can be measured, analyzed, and used as the basis for data-based decisions on institutional improvement. These indicators include the percentage or number of students who

- Complete each developmental education course.
- Take developmental education courses and then enroll in and complete college-level courses.
- Complete gatekeeper courses (usually the first college-level course in a discipline).
- Complete the college courses they take with a grade of *C* or better.
- Enroll from one semester to the next.
- Complete certificates and associate degrees.
- Transfer successfully to 4-year colleges and universities (see Achieving the Dream, 2007).

One additional indicator is the degree to which achievement gaps between targeted students and the general student body have been reduced.

CCSSE (2008) offers an approach to assessing effectiveness by enabling colleges to benchmark performance in comparison to other community colleges. The benchmark areas are the following:

- **Active and collaborative learning.** Students learn more when they are actively involved in their education (asking questions in class, making a class presentation, working with other students, tutoring other students, etc.).
- **Student effort.** The students' own behaviors contribute substantially to their learning (preparing two or more drafts of a paper, using tutorial services, reading assigned books, etc.).
- **Academic challenge**. Challenging intellectual and creative work is central to learning and collegiate quality (meeting high instructor standards, synthesizing and organizing ideas, applying theories or concepts to practical problems or in new situations, etc.).
- **Student–instructor interaction**. The more contact students have with their teachers, the more likely they are to learn effectively and to persist toward achievement of their education goals (communicating with instructors through e-mail, discussing grades or assignments with instructors, seeking feedback from instructors on performance, etc.).
- **Support for learners**. Students perform better and are more satisfied at colleges that are committed to their success and cultivate positive working and social relationships among various groups on campus (providing financial support, providing student support services, facilitating multicultural interactions, etc.).

CLOSING THE ACADEMIC ACHIEVEMENT GAP

By the time many minority students reach high school age, there is a substantial academic achievement gap between them and their White counterparts. There are many causative factors that result in this academic achievement gap—self-limiting individual behaviors, family circumstances (low-income, single-parent families, young mothers, etc.), institutional practices (attendance at low-quality inner-city schools, tracking into less demanding classes, not being assigned to honors and college preparation classes, etc.), and cultural values (negative racial stereotypes, public policy, media portrayal of minorities, etc.).

Community colleges can respond to the inequities that the achievement gap has produced in two primary ways: One, they can work with other community organizations to remedy the cultural and social ills that cause the disparities in wealth and status that underlie the achievement gap (see chapter 7 on reinventing community engagement); and two, they can offer intervention strategies to help individuals overcome the achievement gap, such as financial aid, developmental education, tutorial services, and diversity training for instructors and staff. The goal is to achieve the definition of equity as defined by the Achieving the Dream initiative—not to treat everyone equally, but to provide those services needed by each student and each group of students to empower them to achieve their full potential.

STRATEGIES FOR ENSURING STUDENT SUCCESS

Roueche, Kemper, and Roueche (2006) conducted a study to assess how far community colleges have come in embracing the vision of the learning college. They were disappointed to discover that no colleges could document that they had become learning colleges in their entirety and that there was no indication that the predicted national revolution in learning and teaching reforms was occurring. However, they did identify a number of work-in-progress interventions that appeared to have led to successful implementation, including the following:

- Providing strong and positive administrative and instructor leadership (e.g., instructor leadership in designing and implementing learning outcomes projects, provision of resources and incentives, and improving communications).
- Learning first and last (e.g., funding positions for professionals with extensive training in curriculum and institutional research and creating grassroots learning outcomes committees or teams that develop and implement institutional processes).

Based on a review of several national efforts to promote institutional effectiveness and student success, the most promising interventions by community colleges appear to fall into these categories: developmental education, university transfer, changes in curricula, changes in teaching and learning, student engagement, changes in student support services, changes in instructor roles, and leadership.

Improving Developmental Education

Improving the effectiveness of developmental education programs might be the highest priority for community colleges today. Given the high stakes, what are the emerging best practices? A comprehensive review of effective practices in developmental education conducted by Saxon and Boylan (2001) provided these examples: implementing mandatory student assessment and placement, providing a highly coordinated program, establishing clear objectives and learning outcomes for the program and individual courses, using learning communities, using video-based supplemental instruction, providing tutorial services staffed by well-trained tutors, and providing professional development experiences for those working with underprepared students. According to CCSSE (2005), effective developmental education pays high dividends for underprepared students. It will give students the same chance to complete a degree or transfer to a university as those students who began their studies in college-level courses.

Improving the Transfer Process

Effective transfer processes are critical because community colleges enroll the majority of students who are underrepresented in university student bodies. Today, only about half of community college students whose goal is university transfer actually achieve that goal (Handel, 2009). A more effective transfer program would permit many more students to achieve their full potential and would also have economic and workforce development benefits. Fortunately, institutions like the University of Wisconsin, the University of Maryland, and Cornell and Amherst universities are making efforts to increase the number of low-income transfer students they admit (Handel, 2007). A recent study (Dowd et al., 2006) identified strategies for improved transfer by students from community colleges to universities. From an open-door perspective, promising university practices are the ones that reduce cultural barriers by shaping residence life policies to avoid institutionalized segregation, creating opportunities for welcoming and socializing, and using a variety of assessment strategies to recognize diverse learning styles.

Recent developments also include community colleges offering selected bachelor's degrees, university centers on community college campuses, the availability of online baccalaureate programs, and joint admissions and counseling processes that permit students to achieve early university support and information. Transfer matters are complicated by the "swirl phenomenon," whereby students view education as a commodity and move from institution to institution as needed to meet their specific education goals. There is also the phenomenon of "reverse transfer"—cases in which as many students are transferring from the university to the community college (e.g., to shift to a career education program) as are transferring from the community college to the university.

Adapting Curricula

Curriculum development in the community college has traditionally been the province of the instructors. Although students were often the beneficiaries, a cottage industry emerged in which instructors worked individually or in departmental groups on what interested them. Their priorities might have grown out of identified student and community needs, or they may have grown out of more personal interests such as the focus of their graduate study. In recent years, the curriculum development model has been transformed as colleges and even states have viewed the curriculum as a strategic resource that could be linked to student learning outcomes and the economic and workforce development objectives of the community. We are now seeing the emergence of state-level standard curricula, common state-level course numbering systems, and state-level articulation guides. Regional and specialized accreditation bodies judge academic and career education programs based on their relevance to learning outcomes that match community and workforce needs. College presidents and academic program leaders now view the curriculum, both credit and noncredit, as a strategic resource to be developed and guided by the changing educational needs of students and communities.

Two of the primary areas of interest to college leaders are developmental education and university transfer. Three of the chapters of this book deal with curriculum change as it relates to career education, workforce development, and the linkages with forms of remedial education such as adult education, GED, basic adult education, and high school completion. Other areas of development that respond to the education needs of diverse students are the following:

- The development of online courses to serve a global constituency.
- The focus on gatekeeper courses (usually the first course in a student's major) that, if failed, block progress toward a degree.
- Student success courses on topics such as study skills and time management.
- Dual-enrollment programs that permit high school students to earn a high school diploma while simultaneously getting an early start on earning college credits.
- First-year college programs.
- The introduction of language courses such as Arabic, Chinese, and Japanese in addition to traditional offerings such as German, French, and Spanish.

Adopting New Teaching and Learning Techniques

An amazing array of new teaching and learning strategies is emerging in response to the varying learning styles of the most diverse student body in the history of the community college. That is not to say that the lecture method has been retired; according to the Community College Faculty Survey of Student Engagement (CCSSE , 2006), the majority of instructors still use the lecture as their dominant teaching method. The passive learner—the tired evening student who just wants to sit in the back of the classroom after a busy day at work—is probably still around too. However, recent innovations in teaching and learning tend to center on programs and methods that respond to the varied learning needs and styles of diverse students.

Examples of best practices are provided by the finalists for the MetLife Foundation Community College Excellence Award, which recognizes colleges that implement innovative strategies for helping low-income and first-generation students succeed. Some of the innovative teaching and learning strategies that have been recognized include tutorial centers, special literacy training, and integrated case management for individual students (Allen & Kazis, 2007). Other emerging teaching and learning strategies include distance or online learning; collaborative and interactive strategies such as learning communities, which permit a group of students and instructors to approach learning in an interdisciplinary manner; service learning; work-study experiences tied to the student's discipline; discipline capstone courses; in-class and outside-class student engagement initiatives; supplemental instruction; and computer-aided learning laboratories.

Promoting Student Engagement

Substantial research indicates that students who are actively engaged in their learning are more likely to achieve their education goals than those who are not. For example, CCSSE (2005) found that academically underprepared students take advantage of opportunities for engagement with instructors and counselors slightly more than do academically prepared students. They work harder than they thought they could to meet an instructor's expectations, and they are motivated to write more papers and reports. It is revealing that underprepared students must work harder than academically prepared students to produce similar learning outcomes as they work to overcome the burden of limited literacy skills.

Improving Student Support Services

In the past decade, a number of new student support services have emerged in response to the educational, social, and psychological needs of diverse students. These include outreach to underserved and underprepared students, welcome centers, online admissions and orientation, gender centers, early alert systems to intervene when students are at risk of dropping out, mandatory assessment and course placement, tutorial services, veterans' services, and special needs services (e.g., for people with limited physical capacity). Community colleges must continue to work on the disconnect between instructors and student support services, communications between student support services and academic departments, and the relatively low use of support services by at-risk students. The changing role of student services in response to the needs of diverse students is addressed more fully in chapter 8.

Changing Instructors' Roles

The emergence of the student success dimension of the open-door model has resulted in substantial changes in the role of community college instructors. The role of instructors is becoming more complex and diversified as community colleges place more emphasis on student learning, continuous quality improvement, customer service, and cost control. Examples of how instructors' roles are changing include the following:

- More emphasis on in-class and out-of-class student engagement.
- Use of alternative teaching strategies to respond to diverse learning styles.
- Classroom and course-level assessment of student learning outcomes.
- Increased use of learning technologies both in the classroom and through distance learning.
- More emphasis on collaboration with high school and university counterparts to ease the transition of students from high school to community colleges and from community colleges to universities.
- More emphasis on curriculum improvement based on evidence of gaps in student achievement and the assessment of changing community education needs.
- Greater involvement with instructor professional development activities to keep pace with changing student education needs, societal and economic trends, and learning technologies.
- Stronger connections with library services, student support services, and other departments on behalf of students who experience personal and institutional barriers to success.
- Changing definitions of instructor load in order to balance classroom instruction, curriculum development, student engagement, professional development, departmental service, institutional service, and other professional responsibilities.

Leadership

Chapter 3 outlines the key roles that the college president and other institutional and academic leaders play in reinventing the open door. The core leadership roles relate to the community college mission, college–community interactions, advocacy for underserved and underprepared groups, data-based decision making, and aligning institutional strategy with execution. These leadership roles also center on bringing about systemic, long-term institutional change, such as updating the college mission; updating college policies; shaping the curriculum as a strategic resource tied to changing student and community needs; making changes in administrative, governance, and academic structures; promoting a culture of evidence as it relates to student achievement; building the capacity of instructors and staff to serve the varied education needs of diverse students; and developing holistic diversity, equity, and multicultural programs.

———〰———

Our nation's future economic viability depends on a highly skilled workforce, and the majority of that workforce will be drawn from minority and other population groups that today have the lowest literacy and job skills. Community colleges are being challenged to become a primary force for providing this future workforce with the knowledge and skills needed for job entry and career advancement. Community college leaders fully recognize that a focus on open access to higher education opportunity is not enough to respond to the challenge of the radical demographic, economic, workforce, and cultural transformations facing them. They recognize that a strong emphasis on student success must emerge that builds on the open access tradition and addresses the barriers to career and academic success experienced by students, such as low income, limited literacy and job skills, and other personal factors. They must change core institutional practices so that the achievement gap between targeted students and the general student body can be reduced and eventually eliminated. Many promising student success interventions to achieve these goals are emerging in community colleges throughout the country, and they are being supported in this effort by several universities and national organizations. These interventions actively involve all sectors of the college, including the students, instructors and academic departments, student support services personnel, administrators and support personnel, the president and executive staff, and the governing board.

REFERENCES

Achieving the Dream. (2007). *Success is what counts*. Retrieved from http://www.achievingthedream.org/docs/SUCCESS-counts-FINAL-11.6.pdf

Allen, L., & Kazis, R. (2007). Building a culture of evidence in community colleges. MetLife Foundation. P.

Community College Survey of Student Engagement. (2005). *Engaging students, challenging the odds* [Executive summary]. Available from http://www.ccsse.org/publications/publications.cfm

Community College Survey of Student Engagement. (2006). *Community college survey of faculty engagement*. Available from http://www.ccsse.org/CCFSSE/CCFSSE.cfm

Community College Survey of Student Engagement. (2007). Five lessons learned. In *2007 findings: Executive summary.* Available from http://www.ccsse.org/publications/publications.cfm

Community College Survey of Student Engagement. (2008, July 29). *CCSSE/USA TODAY: Frequently asked questions.* Retrieved from http://www.ccsse.org/USA_Today/CCSSE-USA%20TODAY%20FAQs.pdf

Currie, D. H. (2007). Students: The heart of our community. *Community College Journal, 78*(1), p. 6.

Dowd, A. C., Bensimon , E. M., Gabbard, G., Singleton, S., Macias, E., Dee, J. R., Melguizo, T., Cheslock, J., & Giles, D. (2006). *Transfer access to elite colleges and universities in the United States: Threading the needle of the American dream* [Executive summary]. Boston: University of Massachusetts, Graduate College of Education and New England Resource Center for Higher Education. Available from the Jack Kent Cooke Foundation Web site: http://www.jkcf.org/grants/community-college-transfer/

Handel, S. (2007). Second chance, not second class, a blueprint for community-college transfer. *Change, 39*(5), 38-45.

Handel, S. (2009). Transfer and the part-time student. *Change, 41*(4), 48-53

Roueche, J., Kemper, C., & Roueche, S. (2006). Learning colleges: Looking for revelation but embracing evolution. *Community College Journal, 77*(3), 29-33.

Saxon, D., & Boylan, H. (2001). The cost of remedial education in higher education. *Journal of Developmental Education, 25*(2), 2.

Chapter 6

Campuswide Inclusiveness: Ensuring Equity for Diverse Students

Gunder Myran

The concept of inclusiveness encompasses diversity programs, equity programs, and other multicultural initiatives (e.g., international education, learning communities and other alternative teaching and learning practices, and leadership development programs) to create a community of diverse students, instructors, and staff that will grow together and learn from one another. Community colleges could be viewed as having a new covenant of inclusiveness, diversity, and equity that commits the institution to offering an open door of welcome, affirmation, belonging, and openness for all, and especially for those groups that might otherwise be excluded from opportunities for academic and career mobility.

Another term that is closely aligned to inclusiveness is *equity*. What is an equitable community college? It is not one that treats all students equally, but rather one that provides each student and constituency with the unique services that will empower them to achieve their full potential. The goal of community colleges involved in the Achieving the Dream initiative is to increase student achievement, with a focus on minority and low-income students. Given clear evidence of an achievement gap between Black, Hispanic, and American Indian students compared with the general student body, this is an equitable approach. Many community colleges have equity programs or equity committees charged with helping academic departments to improve student learning outcomes. These programs are a vital part of inclusiveness efforts.

Another key word that relates to inclusiveness is *adaptation*. Traditionally, the student has been required to adapt to the practices of the community college. Class schedules, new courses and programs, and college procedural changes often resulted from instructor and staff interests or convenience rather than the needs of the student. The college program and schedule was communicated to the student, and the student adapted his or her work schedule, child care, family life, and so on, to accommodate the college's mandates. As a result, dealing with issues such as scheduling problems, access to college information, language difficulties, financial concerns, and academic support needs were largely the province of the student, not the college. To the schools' credit and the students' benefit, community colleges have been learning over the past decade to adapt their programs, services, and processes to meet the unique needs of their diverse student body. To be truly inclusive, the community college must be adaptive in response to the changing needs of all students, especially those who experience barriers to career and academic success.

It would be reasonable to ask what common ground community colleges are seeking in shaping an inclusive college environment. This common ground amid diversity could be seen as having three dimensions, as follows:

- **Opportunity for everyone to achieve full potential.** The Mesa Community College (Arizona) policy statement indicates that it serves a diverse population that is reflective of its community and "provides an environment where each individual is respected, honored, supported, and is rewarded on the basis of personal achievement and contribution. Mesa Community College values inclusiveness of people and ideas" (Mesa Community College, 2006).
- **The community college as a living laboratory.** Through developing a deeper appreciation of the differing histories, cultures, and identities of diverse groups, community college students (and instructors and staff as well) are finding common ground; they are learning how to live together in a multicultural society based on the democratic principles of equal justice, social equality, and equal opportunity. A special section of the *Chronicle of Higher Education* (Ashburn, 2006) featured best practices of community colleges in equipping academically at-risk students with the tools to succeed in the global economy. Today's community colleges are a living laboratory of the diverse society in which students live or will certainly live in the future. As students, instructors, and staff learn how to collaborate with their diverse associates in creating an affirming and open environment in which each individual can grow, they can learn to see the world through many lenses, break away from stereotypical and dysfunctional ways of relating, and learn problem-solving skills they will need in a global society.
- **Preparing for a career in a global economy**. The careers of today's community college students will be acted out on the world stage. Through their educational experiences, they must develop an increased awareness of their world and an appreciation of the attributes of various world cultures. They must learn to integrate the values and practices that relate to their own culture with

the values and practices of other cultures. By learning in a community college that has created an inclusive environment, students can develop skills that will serve them as their careers progress.

CREATING A SENSE OF ACCEPTANCE

Any child who has been the last selected when teams choose up sides for a pick-up softball game knows the anxiety that comes from not being accepted and feeling that you do not really belong. We know how painful it is for a teenager to be excluded from a popular clique or to not make the basketball team. Most of us have a need to feel accepted, to be valued, and to belong. When we enter a new environment, it is natural to look for clues as to whether we belong and will be accepted.

The late Max Raines, professor of administration and higher education at Michigan State University, spoke often to me and others about processing losses and gains when entering a new environment. Take, for example, the experience of a single mother with two small children who is admitted to the community college's nursing program. Becoming a nurse will be a definite gain for her, as she will be better able to support herself and her family. However, she experiences the loss of being away from her children, as well as the added cost of a caregiver and uncertainties about the quality of care. Suppose that after a few weeks into the nursing program, her children become ill and the caregiver indicates that it is beyond her capability to care for them. As she processes the gains and losses involved, the student gives priority to her children, thus falling behind in her nursing program. So does she really belong in the nursing program? Of course she does, and an inclusive community college will recognize and be responsive to the unique needs of a single parent in a rigorous nursing program.

In this case, support from nursing instructors and fellow students, financial assistance, and referral and tutorial services will help this single mother over the twin hurdles of caring for her children and progressing in her nursing program. The college says to her in providing these services: "You are accepted as you are, you belong, and you are not alone." Every diverse group that is represented in the community college student body has the same question: Are we really accepted? Do we really belong? When community colleges respond by offering a welcoming, supportive, open learning environment, they are responding in the affirmative, and they are saying that inclusiveness does indeed matter.

A FRAMEWORK OF INCLUSIVENESS

The history of higher education in the United States represents a journey from exclusiveness to inclusiveness, a journey from elite to mass to universal education. Even today, however, there are elements of exclusiveness in the community college environment, such as math and science programs with few minority students, insufficient financial aid programs, teachers unprepared to deal with diversity in the classroom, and an unwelcoming college environment for those who are different from the majority of students. Although the egalitarian ideal of inclusion is deeply rooted in American culture, it is not yet fully realized, even in democracy's college.

Why Inclusiveness Matters: A Tribute to a Community College Instructor

The late Morris Lawrence was a founding faculty member at Washtenaw Community College (Michigan). He was a beloved music instructor and a talented musician. He loved his work, and he loved his students. He stopped his car on the way to work each morning to pray that he would work so hard for his students that the sweat would run down his back. He drew to his music classes many students who would not otherwise have considered a higher education. He treated every student with respect and caring, regardless of their race, ethnicity, or socioeconomic status. He nurtured the careers of his students by involving them in community music groups. His jazz orchestra was selected to perform at venues such as Carnegie Hall in New York City and the Montrose Jazz Festival in Detroit. Such was his lasting impact on the college that there is today a Morris Lawrence Building on campus. An annual award is given in his name to an instructor who exemplifies his loving spirit with students and his devotion to teaching. The Morris Lawrence story indicates that inclusiveness really does matter, and it is most directly expressed when dedicated and caring teachers, counselors, and staff acknowledge value and nurture students regardless of their background.

— *Gunder Myran, former president,*
Washtenaw Community College

It is no doubt generally true that public higher education, including the community college sector, has historically been dominated and shaped by the White middle-class culture. In the spirit of the melting pot, those of other racial and ethnic origins were to be assimilated into the dominant White culture, primarily through the instrument of public education. As a result, the cultural identities of other racial, ethnic, and socioeconomic groups were marginalized in the community college as well as in the larger society. From an education perspective, this acculturation process resulted in a limited and distorted worldview for both White and minority students and, in fact, for the college instructors and staff as well.

In recent years, however, community colleges have been struggling to develop a more inclusive multicultural framework through which people from varied backgrounds can express their identities and education goals. This commitment to inclusiveness is becoming a defining feature of community colleges. Through their actions to become more inclusive, community colleges are redefining the open door of education opportunity and reaffirming their commitment to democratic principles.

The framework of inclusiveness represents a positive web of interaction between the diverse people and divergent viewpoints represented in the college and the community it serves. This emerging framework has two major dimensions. The first is the internal struggle of the college itself to become more inclusive and democratic and, in doing so, to redefine what a community college education is to achieve for people who will live out their lives in a pluralistic and multicultural society. Second is the efforts of the community college to be engaged with other organizations and groups to create a more inclusive, democratic, just, humane, and socially responsible community. The framework is based on a review of best practices of community colleges as they develop their inclusiveness agenda and consists of eight elements, described in the following paragraphs.

1. The Spirit of the Open Door

Community college professionals believe strongly that talent and ambition are widely distributed in our society rather than being the province of an elite few. This belief is founded on participating in the everyday miracles of students who achieve great things against all odds. For community college professionals, being inclusive means including those who have two strikes against them, those who logic might suggest are at high risk of failure—high school dropouts, single parents on welfare, alienated Black youths, the unemployed, people who have emotional and mental problems, and so on. This attitude of hopefulness—confidence that people can rise above their present status in life and achieve beyond expectations by overcoming barriers to academic and career success—captures the community college spirit. It is this spirit that drives and animates community college efforts to become more inclusive as waves of people from all demographic groups seek academic and career success.

2. Diversity Programs

Many community colleges have diversity programs, and, in some cases, a diversity office exists and a diversity officer has been appointed. The functions and activities of diversity programs vary widely, but they can include activities such as instructor and staff hiring practices, professional development, multicultural curricula, diversity courses, task forces or workshops on race and racism, cultural events celebrating various cultural traditions, art exhibits, visiting scholars and artists, collegewide town hall meetings on diversity topics, diversity assessments or surveys, and special programs to bring diverse groups together.

3. Curriculum and Teaching and Learning

Recent developments include multicultural programming, the expansion of international education programs including international travel, ESL programs, freshmen-year programs focusing on retention, learning communities and other classroom teambuilding methods, teaching and learning centers, recognition of differing communications styles (e.g., instructor–student and student–student communications) based on cultural origins, and special cultural programs for specific constituencies (e.g., Hispanic, American Indian, and other minority students).

4. Student Services

Recent developments in student services include expanded recruitment of at-risk constituencies, special scholarship programs, case management of at-risk students, student diversity advocates, special semester startup welcome-back activities, and mentoring and tutorial services.

5. Faculty and Staff Development

Recent developments include collegewide human resources and diversity strategic planning, modified affirmative action programs, modified instructor and staff hiring practices, new forms of instructor and staff orientation, and diversity-oriented instructor and staff professional development.

6. Leadership and Administration

Recent developments include recognition of an inclusiveness, diversity, and equity commitment in colleges' mission and vision statements; updated inclusiveness policies; inclusiveness strategic and management planning; structural changes such as the appointment of a diversity officer; appointment of access and equity advisory committees; inclusion-oriented leadership development programs; special funding of inclusiveness practices through college foundations; reallocation of financial resources to address inclusiveness issues; annual executive inclusiveness retreats; inclusive governance practices; and inclusiveness recognition and awards.

7. High-Quality Learning Conditions

California Tomorrow (2002) conducted a study of the high-quality learning conditions needed to support students of color and immigrants at California community colleges. They concluded that the following conditions are needed:

- **Better mechanisms for accessing information and counseling.** Students struggle with issues such as how to apply for admissions, decide which classes to take, sign up for classes, and find out about support services. Peer networks and the advice of teachers were considered helpful, but the most important factor was the availability of a qualified professional counselor.

- **Qualified instructors with the skills to teach a linguistically and culturally diverse population.** Teachers can be the greatest influence for students in college—either positive and validating or negative and invalidating. Students value interactive and hands-on teaching strategies, and they want learning that is relevant to their daily lives. Students considered the accessibility of teachers both in and outside the classroom an important factor.

- **Greater financial aid and other supports for community college students.** Students need support in balancing family, work, and study. Financial support is critical, but taking the number of credit hours required to be eligible for financial aid in some community colleges is often unrealistic. Those who attempt full-time study often experience stress, fall behind, and drop out. The majority of students need developmental education, but the success rate in these courses indicates the need for major improvements. Students considered supplemental academic support—such as tutorial centers, learning communities, instructor availability during office hours, and bilingual language support services beyond ESL programs—important.

- **Welcoming, supportive campus atmospheres for immigrant minority students**. Students in the study often flourished in the supportive atmosphere of their campus, finding joy in learning for the first time in their lives. At the same time, however, they also experienced invalidating attitudes and disrespect, rudeness, and negative stereotypes on the part of counselors, teachers, and staff. Students were encouraged by those teachers who conducted cultural awareness activities in their classes or who included sections on other cultures in their courses.

- **Targeted resources and support programs**. The most effective supplemental support services were those closely linked to a course or program, not a separate program. Students were strongly supportive of learning communities, adequate financial aid, child care, book and transportation vouchers, counseling, good information services, personal development workshops, in-depth first-year orientation, and tutorial services. Students appreciated the opportunity to develop an ongoing relationship with a staff member providing supplemental support.

- **Instructor diversity and sensitivity**. The majority of students felt that diverse instructors were beneficial to them. At some colleges, there was a need to develop a more effective strategy for recruiting diverse instructors and staff. Effective diversity-oriented professional development for instructors and staff on how to work with diverse students was considered important.

8. Community Engagement

This element of the framework extends the inclusiveness agenda beyond the borders of the college and into the larger community. Old community engagement models and practices are simply incapable of casting a wide enough net to be truly inclusive for all community constituencies that need to be served, and so the way community colleges engage with their communities is being reframed. Some recent developments in this reframing process include expanded public school–community college transition programs, involvement in the middle college and charter school movements, partnerships with community-based organizations serving at-risk populations, partnerships with prisons and the court system, community summits on critical community issues such as the urban Black family, participation in the Campus Compact program, youth leadership training, and health screening services. The emerging community engagement model of community colleges is addressed in more detail in chapter 7.

BEST PRACTICES FOR IMPLEMENTING THE INCLUSIVENESS AGENDA

Some of the best practices of community colleges that can serve as examples for implementing the inclusiveness agenda are the following:

- Seattle Central Community College was featured in *Time* magazine (Goldstein, 2009) for its learning communities program and other innovative initiatives. Seattle Central's learning communities are interdepartmental groupings that promote teamwork and problem solving among teams of students from varied demographic groups.
- Several community colleges are targeting close-to-retirement baby boomers who wish to make a career transition. Central Florida Community College provides a Pathways to Living, Learning and Serving program. Central Piedmont Community College in North Carolina provides Career Transition at Midlife and What's Next seminars, and Chandler-Gilbert Community College in Arizona provides a Boomerang program of lifelong learning opportunities.
- The San Diego Community College District has pushed inclusiveness to include the lost generation of high school students who dropped out of high school and failed to graduate in 2006. According to Beebe (2007), "The educational system has tagged many of these young people as failures. They have broken spirits and broken lives. Most are unemployed or unemployable. People of color represent a disproportionate percentage of the lost generation." Beebe highlighted the district's continuing education division and its accredited adult high school. To help high school dropouts see the connec-

tion between education and work, the department links basic skills education with career technical education in areas such as welding, auto repair, health care, and culinary arts. By adapting its programs and services to the unique needs of this at-risk constituency, the San Diego Community College District is reaffirming the worth of these students and giving them a sense of belonging and accomplishment.

⸻ ❧ ⸻

As a community college creates a welcoming, affirming, and open environment, students, instructors, and staff are empowered to express their unique identities as they together strive for the common good. The inclusiveness agenda provides students with the experience of working with and relating to others in a multicultural learning environment that models how effective communities and workplaces should function. It prepares students for the world of work by giving them a heightened sense of awareness and appreciation of the cultures of those from diverse demographic backgrounds with whom they will collaborate as their careers progress. Inclusiveness is the connecting thread that brings the entire community college family together as a unified whole and enables it to carry out its open-door mission.

REFERENCES

Ashburn, E. (2006, October 27). Living laboratories: 5 community colleges offer lessons that have produced results. *Chronicle of Higher Education.* Retrieved from http://chronicle.com/chronicle/v53/5310guide.htm

Beebe, A.E. (2007 April/May). Saving the lost generation. *Community College Journal,* 18–23.

California Tomorrow. (2002, April 1). *The high-quality learning conditions needed to support students of color and immigrants at California Community Colleges* [Policy report]. Paper presented at the California Joint Legislation Committee, Sacramento, CA. (ERIC # ED 465383)

Goldstein, A. (2009). Seattle Central. *TIME.com.* Retrieved from http://www.time.com/time/2001/coy/community.html

Mesa Community College. (2006). *Diversity.* Retrieved from http://www.mc.maricopa.edu/about/administration/president/diversity/

Chapter 7

Community-Based Problem Solving to Maximize Community Engagement

George Swan

uth Shaw, former president of Central Piedmont Community College in Charlotte, North Carolina, tells a story about offering a ride home to a student after an evening scholarship reception at the college. They left a reception in a lovely dining room that featured tiny sandwiches on silver trays to travel to the student's home in an inner-city neighborhood with run-down housing and urban blight. "There is a vast distance from her life in the shadow of Charlotte to classrooms at CPCC to the career toward which she aspires," Shaw said (cited in Elliot, 1994, p. 50). Writing for *Change* magazine, Margaret Miller referred to the public responsibility for disparities in educational performance when she said the following:

> The disparities in educational performance of the various subcultures
> of this country in areas such as college matriculation, learning and
> degree completion didn't just happen, they were created. And we
> continue to continue to create them every day by the policies,
> both institutional and public, we develop or fail to develop. (Miller,
> 2007, p. 6)

The questions addressed in this chapter relate to the public responsibility for disparities in the academic performance of diverse students and the distance or disconnect between a nurturing community college environment and the dysfunctional communities in which many students live. How do community colleges effect changes that reduce the social, economic, and psychological distance between community life and student success on the college campus? How do they contribute to social change that reduces barriers to career and academic success for diverse students, barriers such as poverty, unemployment, family dysfunction, substandard housing, urban decay, crime, and racism?

At a 2006 national conference at Wayne County Community College District (WCCCD) on reinventing the community college open door, noted author on social innovation David Bornstein urged leaders to have faith in new possibilities and the courage to advocate them as they address social and economic problems in the communities they serve. Bornstein said that we have a mission-driven obligation to be deeply involved in community change strategies. He encouraged conference participants to emulate social entrepreneurs around the world who brought about fundamental changes in their communities or countries through the power of new ideas and an entrepreneurial spirit. In his book, *How to Change the World,* Bornstein stated that social entrepreneurship "takes creative individuals with fixed determination and indomitable will to propel the innovations that society needs to tackle its toughest problems" (Bornstein, 2007, p. 3). Bornstein suggested, for example, innovations such as sponsoring and training students from the inner city, who then become social entrepreneurs themselves and address problems in their own neighborhoods as a part of their collegiate program.

TYPES OF COMMUNITY ENGAGEMENT

Community engagement is the community college's approach to public leadership that uses the college's education resources to solve problems in cooperation with citizens and other organizations. Through a framework of services and connections, the college is deeply embedded in the daily life of the community. It serves as a value-driven force for the public good and for addressing conditions that represent barriers to career and academic success for diverse students. Social entrepreneurship is a form of engagement in which students, instructors, and staff of the community college use powerful social-change ideas to increase and mobilize the capacity of citizens to solve their own problems. Social entrepreneurship occurs through volunteerism, instructional programming, student activities, internships, and work-study arrangements.

Organizations across the nation collaborate to support the colleges' open-door philosophy. Among those whose focus complements our mission, one recurring theme is that education is a key to success for individuals as well as for the larger community. As they partner to fulfill their individual missions, their philanthropic vigor furthers the goals of community colleges nationwide. Despite genuine efforts to improve access to higher education, a compelling and powerful mission alone is not sufficient. The organizations work together to fund and support dozens of initiatives and programs that are supported by research, pursued through innovation, and measured for effectiveness. A current and expanding theme in community colleges centers on student engagement in the community, with roots in the cooperative extension movement at the University of Cincinnati in 1903. The current literature is replete with reports on strategies, testimonies, and research on effective and best practices for student engagement. It is an expanding movement, with public and private resources devoted to encouraging, stimulating, seeding, and sustaining student engagement projects.

The Corporation for National and Community Service (2006) has made an annual commitment of more than $150 million to expand service learning and campus volunteering through grants. The strategic plan of the corporation sets a national target to increase the number of college students in community engagement projects from 3.2 million students in 2005 to 5 million students by 2010. The National Service-Learning Clearinghouse lists on its Web site (http://www.service-learning.org) grant opportunities, links, and publications that describe opportunities for rural, urban, tribal, Hispanic, doctoral research, local, state, and regional collaborative projects as well as funding for research on student community engagement. There is also growing attention on the part of regional accrediting associations and organizations—such as the Carnegie Foundation for the Advancement of Teaching, the National Survey of Student Community Engagement, and the Community College Survey of Student Engagement—to establish and influence institutional measures that stimulate and promote community engagement initiatives.

The Carnegie Foundation, for example, conducted an extensive revision of the Carnegie Classification of Institutions of Higher Education, providing an elective classification for community engagement defined as "the collaboration between institutions of higher education and their larger communities (local, regional and state, national, global) for the mutually beneficial exchange of knowledge and resources in a context of partnership and reciprocity" (Carnegie Foundation, 2007). In 2006, 88 institutions applied to Carnegie to document community engagement, seeking classification in one of the following three categories of the new framework:

- **Curricular engagement**. Defined as "teaching, learning, and scholarship that engages faculty, students and community in mutually beneficial and respectful collaboration" (Carnegie Foundation, 2007).
- **Outreach and partnerships**. Described as "the application and provision of institutional resources for community use with benefits to both campus and community" and "collaborative interactions with community and related scholarship for the mutually beneficial exchange, exploration, and application of knowledge, information, and resources" (Carnegie Foundation, 2007).
- **Curricular engagement and outreach and partnerships**. Focused on institutions with substantial commitments in both areas.

Organizations such as Campus Compact, a national coalition of nearly 1,100 colleges and universities representing some 6 million students, are dedicated to promoting community service, civic engagement, and service learning in higher education. Student engagement in the community has become an expectation for many institutions in the development of inter- and intra-curricular experiences for learning and training. Centers for community engagement are now active on many college campuses, with a great deal of time and effort devoted to recruiting students and soliciting opportunities for service-learning experiences.

In some instances, institutional policies and standards have been modified, necessitating contractual agreements by students for volunteer service in exchange for academic credit or to meet a requirement for graduation. This is in addition to the practica, clinicals, and internships traditionally associated with career and technical programs. Although most service-learning projects have originated in 4-year colleges and universities, an increasing number of community colleges have instituted student engagement projects.

ADOPTING A NEW FRAMEWORK

There is a need to recognize and celebrate the development of student engagement programs in communities served by 2-year colleges. The testimonies of student volunteers in the transformation of lives touched through interaction and intervention in communities where these initiatives have been developed are evidence of their positive effect. It is a great lesson for the students who have had the experience. Yet, there is another powerful lesson that emerges from their experience. The social benefits of student engagement in communities can transform the impact that colleges have in those same communities, by shaping new opportunities and opening access for those entering the colleges' new open door. It is an important lesson that college leaders seeking to strengthen the strategic positioning of their colleges should note, because it serves their own best interests as well as the communities they serve to address the barriers to higher education that are often related to the same issues and problems that communities themselves would like to address and resolve.

Driven by this common ground for the community college and its community partners, a reframing of community engagement objectives and programs is occurring. This reframing is based on the recognition that old community engagement models and practices are simply incapable of casting a wide enough net to be truly inclusive for all community constituencies that need to be served. Some recent developments in this reframing process include expanded public school–community college transition programs, involvement in the middle college and charter school movements, partnerships with community-based organizations serving at-risk populations, partnerships with prisons and the court system, community summits on critical community issues such as the urban Black family, participation in the Campus Compact program, youth leadership training, and health screening services.

SOCIAL BENEFIT AND RECIPROCATION

A goal of providing service-learning experiences for students is to promote awareness, commitment, and a perspective favorable to helping and serving others. Student involvement in such projects is cited as contributing to the health and well-being of communities. If student engagement serves a social benefit, then the need for community college engagement in those same communities becomes even more notable—especially in the context of intervention, collaboration, and partnerships with local organizations and groups. Although this is not to suggest that colleges should become involved in direct service activities that are beyond their capacity, collaboration between colleges and community organizations can increase affinity and identification among those who are affected by the effort.

The perceived interdependence of such collaborations serves to benefit colleges, given the likelihood that recipients of services and assistance will demonstrate a preference for and affinity toward the college. This is true not only for themselves but also as they serve as advocates encouraging family and friends to use their community's college. Collaboration between community organizations and colleges can also support a reciprocal relationship, enabling student access to services that the college is unable to provide. At a time when colleges are confronted with determining priorities given to programs and services in the competition for scarce resources, such a reciprocal relationship is appealing—even given the challenge to expand and enhance the offerings and support systems demanded by increasing numbers of students of the open-door community college. Such an arrangement broadens the array of supportive services and assistance that members of the collaborative can offer to their respective constituencies. It enables community colleges faced with the myriad issues confronting diverse students to offer realistic approaches to supporting their matriculation at the college.

PUBLIC COLLEGES AND RETURN ON INVESTMENT

A common measure for investors to determine the benefit of their investment is a calculation of the ROI. Although an economic impact statement is more often used by colleges to demonstrate the effect of their presence and operations in a community for the public good, the results cannot be personalized to the extent that the observer perceives a direct benefit. They are typically directed at an informed community for political or funding purposes, whether seeking support for state or county appropriations, allocations, or public referenda for voter-approved assessments.

Yet the people who most desire to understand the role and benefit that the community college offers are often those who seek its services or assistance. For students of the open-door community college, the ability of colleges to effectively convey the ROI must be related to access and opportunities that are constructive and transformative. For those in the larger community, there is a need to engender personal identification of the college as a substantial partner in the fabric of the community. If there is merit in requiring student engagement in community activities in order to provide a benefit to the greater society, community colleges as public entities must be equally focused on the ROI owed to area residents, the public and private sectors, region, and state. To use the vernacular, we need to practice what we preach. If community engagement is great for students, it is likewise good for colleges and our communities. As a strategy to convey the effect of a college in the service area, institutional community engagement may be the method through which the ROI is best personalized and understood.

Why is community engagement at the institutional level important? Is it altruism, strategic positioning, or both? One might ask, Isn't it obvious that a community college, by design, seeks to meet the needs of the surrounding community by offering programs and services promoting the economic, social, cultural, and workforce needs of its district? Is it not the case that community colleges are organized around mission statements founded on the social benefit to their constituents? Is it reasonable to assume that a college could sustain critical funding through state appropriations (and, in some cases, local tax assessments) if not serving a vital role to the public? If students from a community college are involved in service-learning projects, is it not the case that the community understands that the relationship was promulgated by the college and the positive benefit is linked directly to the college?

The issue is a pragmatic one. All public 2-year institutions face pressure on a number of levels to validate and justify their use of taxpayer funds. If they are part of a state system, they need a larger allocation of appropriated funds. If they are in local taxing districts, they must convince voters that they are worthy of continued support for their assessment. The increasing demand for accountability and transparency of outcome measures by federal, state, and local authorities, along with regional accrediting associations, is a constant factor in the demand for evidence of the value and significance of colleges in serving a vital role for their communities. Senior administrators must illustrate the value of community colleges to their constituencies. The ability to develop a base of grassroots advocates enhances a college's standing among those who are in turn asked to show their support in the voting booth.

Whatever the college's response may be in mandated reporting to government and regulatory agencies, the strategic question raised by those who are potential advocates for their local community college is reflected in the question "What have you done for me lately?" It is a question often raised by citizens, legislators, and other interests in the competition for resources in an increasingly constrained fiscal environment. More and more, the question is being raised along with greater competition for limited resources on all levels. Are we seeking the strategic positioning necessary to effectively address the question? What makes a college distinct from others in justifying an advantage in the competition for resources? If each organization delivers the same quality and range of traditional services, what makes it exceptional to its constituents? Community engagement might be an effective strategy.

IMPROVING SUPPORT FOR COMMUNITY PRIORITIES

Students cannot serve adequately as proxies in addressing the question of a college's commitment through their community service and engagement. When measured against the visibility, prestige, and resources implicit in an institutional commitment in support of a community program or initiative, students engaged in service-learning projects do not carry the same weight of influence that other community leaders do. What are the consequences if institutions are not seen as supportive of community initiatives or priorities? Is it sufficient to simply restate and illuminate the mission and purpose to serve a public benefit as justification for continued community support? Or does the need rise to a different level?

In the great growth period of public 2-year colleges between 1950 and the mid-1970s, the sense of excitement, purpose, and benefit of these new comprehensive colleges seemed apparent. The accessibility, flexibility, and convenience of colleges devoted to the ideals of social uplift, economic development, and the democratization of postsecondary education transfixed the public. During that period, the rising subscription of programs and course offerings necessitated investment in buildings, campuses, and technologies to accommodate student needs.

Given the maturation of 2-year public colleges some 40 years later and the wide array of options now available for students to gain the necessary competencies and skill sets through a variety of learning modalities, the future of the community college must borrow from its past and include a strong emphasis on community engagement. The public 2-year college cannot aspire to be an ivory tower; rather, the comprehensive community college must be able to demonstrate the effect of its presence for those living and working in its district. If it does not, the response to the question "What have you done for me lately?" is insufficient to garner the public support necessary for the future.

This was the challenge for WCCCD many years ago when there was the need to seek support for a local tax assessment to augment college operations. The development of an institutional community engagement strategy was fundamental to the success of that campaign (WCCCD, 2009). The effort to create an appropriate context for a favorable response to the ballot initiative was exceptional given the economic climate, the rejection of several local public school initiatives, and voter turnout in special elections. The confidence expressed in the community college was, in part, proportional to the benefit that voters perceived in programs and services that they and their family members, neighbors, and friends could expect. Although some might suggest that a good marketing campaign could generate the same result, the ability to build and sustain a coterie of third-party advocates demands a greater investment. What are the lessons learned from this experience, and how can an institution gain affirmation within its district? First, define community engagement as a part of the strategic plan, and second, expand the definition of institutional engagement beyond the ranks of senior leaders to empower community engagement entrepreneurs.

DEFINE COMMUNITY ENGAGEMENT AS PART OF THE STRATEGIC PLAN

Engagement cannot be limited to a series of classes offered through the continuing education department or the occasional public event on campus. Engagement must become an integral part of the college's intent, planning, and operations. To be meaningful, it must be inculcated throughout the organization as a principal aspect of the mission actualized by the inclusion in the budget of allocated resources. The classification framework for the Carnegie Foundation includes the following indicators of an institution's commitment to community engagement:

- Does the institution indicate that community engagement is a priority in its mission statement (or vision)?
- Does the institution have mechanisms for systematic assessment of community perceptions of the institution's engagement with community?
- Is community engagement emphasized in the marketing materials (Web site, brochures, etc.) of the institution?
- Does the executive leadership of the institution (president, provost, chancellor, trustees, etc.) explicitly promote community engagement as a priority?
- Are there internal budgetary allocations dedicated to supporting institutional engagement with community?
- Is there external funding dedicated to supporting institutional engagement with community?
- Is community engagement defined and planned for in the strategic plans of the institution? (Carnegie Foundation, 2007)

These questions are extracted from the Foundational Indicators section of the framework document. The ways in which leaders of community colleges answer these questions demonstrate whether community engagement is part of an ongoing dialogue—a meaningful commitment to their communities as partners and collaborators for the public good. This is not to suggest an all-or-nothing approach in measuring institutional commitment. Rather, the process of integrating institutional engagement is intentional and directive, not a response to what is the current fad or fashion. In taking the measured steps to weave institutional community engagement into the fabric of the college, leaders ensure the viability (and therefore a legacy) of collaboration with constituents beyond their own tenure.

EXPAND THE DEFINITION OF ENGAGEMENT BEYOND THE RANKS OF SENIOR LEADERS

The participation of senior leaders in local organizations, boards, and community events has long defined community engagement. It has been assumed that such engagement with local schools, businesses, and corporate partners, along with the input and contributions offered by program and campus advisory boards, is an adequate measure of involvement with external audiences. Involvement in the governance of local agencies and associations, meetings with media representatives, and community activities provide sufficient opportunities for leaders to gauge public sentiment and derive input on the important issues facing the community college. The advice and direction for the college in meeting community needs is therefore made available to senior leaders, and it might even be captured to use in testimonial statements of support, published reports, and public presentations. However, that input often remains limited to a small network surrounding the senior leadership group. Institutional engagement, if it is to be meaningful, must extend beyond the ranks of senior leaders.

This is not to disparage contributions by college leaders as a visible presence for their institutions in the communities that they serve. Certainly, one could cite numerous exceptional efforts across the nation by those in the higher echelons of institutions networking with other leaders in their service areas to create positive rapport and build constructive relations. It is a responsibility of those to whom the institution has been entrusted to develop a high level of personal contact with constituents. However, the concept of institutional engagement compels everyone in the college's internal community to take leadership roles on the outside. Instructors and staff can also help to define opportunities for beneficial and reciprocal relationships in the community and can participate in the development of partnerships and collaborative efforts. In essence, colleges should seek to empower those within the college who have the interest to become community engagement entrepreneurs. This is not to suggest that colleges turn staff and instructors loose to develop relationships on their own without a corresponding structure or preparation. Instead, leaders should provide instructors and staff with training and professional development to support institutional community engagement priorities and include instructors and staff from the outset in developing and designing engagement programs to strengthen the presence of the college within the community.

College leaders must see community engagement as going beyond providing opportunities for students to perform community service. Institutional community engagement is necessary and vital in serving the needs of diverse students as well as the environment from which they come. The complexities of the communities served and the resources available to support and promote learning are limited and constrained, but they can be enhanced and increased through beneficial and reciprocal collaborative relationships with community partners. Leaders must extend the responsibility for engagement beyond the upper echelon of college administrators by building roles for community engagement entrepreneurs at all levels. The viability of the comprehensive community college is to make real the aspect of community in its mission, vision, and strategic intent. Only then will these institutions be truly responsive and engaged as the community's colleges.

REFERENCES

Bornstein, D. (2007). *How to change the world: Social entrepreneurship and the power of new ideas.* New York, NY: Oxford University Press.

Carnegie Foundation for the Advancement of Teaching. (2007, October 23). *Effective classification: Community engagement. 2008 documentation framework.* Retrieved from http://www.carnegiefoundation.org/dynamic/downloads/file_1_614.pdf

Corporation for National and Community Service. (2006). *Strategic plan 2006–2010.* Retrieved from http://www.nationalservice.gov/pdf/strategic_plan_web.pdf

Elliott, P. G. (1994). *The urban campus: Educating the new majority for the new century.* Phoenix, AZ: American Council on Education and Oryx Press. (ERIC # ED 372154)

Miller. M. A. (2007, March/April). Falling between the cracks [Editorial]. *Change.*

Wayne County Community College District. (2009). *Strategic plan 2003–2008.* Detroit, MI: Wayne County Community College, Office of the Chancellor. Retrieved from http://www.wcccd.edu/dept/pdf/IE/strategic_plan.pdf

Chapter 8

Reinventing Student Services for Today's Diverse Students

Carol Wells

ahlil Gibran wrote in *The Prophet* that "Work is love made visible" (1970, p. 32). This statement captures well the spirit and values that are the foundation of the work of student services professionals in community colleges. Student services professionals often speak of their love for the students they serve, their love of service to others, and their joy when students overcome barriers to career and academic success. In the past decade, this commitment to the welfare and success of each student has been tested as student services divisions have been challenged to respond to the variety and complexity of needs and problems presented by an increasingly diverse student body. During this period, the caring concern for each student, regardless of race, ethnicity, gender, socioeconomic status, and other personal attributes, has been the driving force for transformational changes in student services. This passion for dramatic and meaningful change is based on the recognition that today's diverse students are characteristic of our pluralistic society and the belief that this pluralism is the very essence of our democracy.

The emerging mission of student services divisions in community colleges in response to diverse students has three dimensions:

- Providing specific academic, personal, social, and career support services to empower students from diverse backgrounds to gain college access and achieve their career and academic goals.
- Leading the development of a campuswide environment of inclusiveness that

welcomes, appreciates, and supports people of all backgrounds.
- Serving as a collegewide catalyst and advocate for infusing learner-centered perspectives and practices into all stages of college and for the integration and coordination of student-centered activities across all divisions and programs of the college.

Historically, student services in the community college have been somewhat isolated from the mainstream instructional divisions, and, at times, they have played a marginalized role within the college (e.g., the first to sustain budget cuts). Student services leaders were seen as overseeing important operational services such as student admissions and class registration, but they did not tend to have a powerful voice in strategy discussions. Also, the connection between student services professionals and instructors has not always been strong, with some instructors being unaware of specific student services and rarely having contact with counselors and other student services providers.

As increasingly diverse students have entered the classroom and laboratory, instructors may have also felt isolated as they coped, seemingly alone, with the challenges of poorly prepared students, such as those with limited language skills, physical limitations, and mental health issues. To build bridges between the academic and student services dimensions of the college, student services leaders are now thinking strategically and collaboratively as they work with instructors and academic leaders to create a seamless learning environment that supports the academic and personal development of a diverse student body. In addition, in recent years, presidents and other college leaders have recognized the importance of involving student services leaders in forums about the colleges' strategic directions.

THE IMPETUS FOR CHANGE IN STUDENT SERVICES

Most students enrolling in community colleges have at least one of several risk factors that include delayed postsecondary enrollment, part-time attendance, lack of financial support, having dependents, being a single parent, having no high school diploma, and working full time while enrolled. The special needs of the following constituencies have been identified as being important factors in driving change in college services:

- adult learners
- international students
- distance learning students
- first-generation college students
- students with learning disabilities
- single parents with small children

- dual- or concurrent-enrollment high school students
- students with emotional or mental problems
- students with physical limitations
- high school dropouts
- Hispanic students

Of those constituencies, the first four are probably having perhaps the greatest effect.

- **Adult learners**. The effects of a changing society and changing economic conditions have resulted in an increasing number of students 25 years old and older enrolling in a formal collegiate course of study, the majority of them on a part-time basis. The term *adult learner* includes a broad spectrum of groups, including women, immigrants, second-career retirees, and single parents with young children.
- **International students.** Community colleges have seen a substantial increase in the number of international students enrolled. Although much of this increase is attributable to the information available on the Internet, international students have found community colleges desirable because of the obvious financial benefits compared with the tuition of 4-year colleges and universities.
- **Distance learning students**. New technologies have removed the geographical barriers of attending a local community college, thereby allowing students to take online classes anywhere in the world. Distance learning is revolutionizing higher education, and it has major implications for the delivery of student services. Providing 24/7 online support services to distance learning students is critical not only from the students' perspective but also from the schools' perspective. By maintaining a strong package of 24/7 online services with admissions, registration, advising, and tutoring, colleges are developing the capacity to serve the growing number of students who elect to take courses online. (For a more detailed description of the uses of technology in student services, see chapter 9.)
- **First-generation college students.** First-generation college students are more likely to be women, older, employed full time, take fewer credits each semester, and depend on financial aid as a major source of financial support. Like other adult learners, these students often experience a number of personal and financial problems that present obstacles to the completion of their education goals. First-generation college students are more likely to attend a community college to improve their job skills rather than to transfer to a 4-year college or university.

Table 8.1 Traditional and New Services to Accommodate Diverse Students

Traditional Student Services	New Student Services
• Academic advising	• Family support services
• Admissions	• First year of college program
• Assessment and testing	• Gender centers
• Career counseling and job placement	• Learning communities
• Child care	• Multicultural, diversity, and equity programs
• College or study skills programs	• One-stop service centers (student-friendly integration of student services)
• Counseling and mental health services	• Online 24/7 services (admissions, orientation, registration, etc.) for all students
• Early alert (early intervention in cases of student attendance lapses, etc.)	• Online 24/7 services for distance learning students
• Financial aid	• Outreach to schools (on-campus days for middle school students, Saturday academy for girls, minority achievement programs, child–parent college awareness days, summer bridge programs, etc.)
• Graduation services	
• Marketing and student recruitment	
• Orientation	
• Registration and class placement	• Program collaboration with academic departments (developmental education, learning communities, etc.)
• Service partnerships with universities and public schools	• Service partnerships with social agencies, churches, nonprofit organizations, etc.
• Special services for students with limited physical capacity	• Summer bridge programs
• Student activities (student clubs, publications, special events, etc.)	• Transition programs for school dropouts, adult education students, adjudicated youth, etc.
• Student employment (work-study)	• Welcome centers (precollege advising, campus tours, financial aid assistance, new student days, new student orientation, etc.)
• Student exit interviews and follow-up studies	
• Student housing services	
• Student records	
• Student retention services	
• Support and self-help groups	
• Tutorial and mentoring services	
• University transfer services	
• Veterans services	

STRATEGIC AREAS OF CHANGE IN STUDENT SERVICES

Table 8.1 provides a snapshot of a moving target: the evolving array of student services being modified or introduced in response to the changing needs of a diverse student body. The first column lists traditional services that nevertheless are going through ongoing modification, and the second column lists services that have emerged or have been transformed in recent years. Four areas of strategic change are occurring in student services as community colleges respond to the personal and academic needs of diverse students, as described in the following sections.

Integrated Student Services

The traditional model of student services consisted of separately defined services intended to facilitate academic and career success. On most campuses, services such as admissions, assessment, orientation, registration, advising, records, academic support, career placement, and graduation services exist as separate offices or functions. Students must first determine which of these services they need and then travel from one office or person to another to access the service. Organizationally, the structure reflects segregated processes. There is often limited communication from one department or function to the next as well as limited access to the academic functions of the college. With the emergence of more diverse students, technology, overall enrollment growth, and emphasis on customer service and student learning outcomes, community colleges must now respond with a more integrated approach to the delivery of services. The interaction among all functions and programs is critical to quality. The system of services must be connected, collaborative, comprehensive, and organized in a barrier-free, student-friendly fashion.

An example of an integrated approach is the council structure used by Wayne County Community College District (Detroit, MI). Every major college division maintains a council with members from all other divisions of the college—finance, education affairs, workforce and continuing education, information technology, college effectiveness, and distance learning. All representatives have a direct effect on the services provided to students. Issues discussed and resolved at the council meetings range from tuition payments to transferring credit. Communication is open, and the process of changing policy or modifying practices is expedited. The council deliberates and makes recommendations on both strategic and operational matters, thereby integrating decisions on the improvement of student services with those of other divisions of the college.

Collegewide Advocacy

Because the values of student services center on caring concern for each student, the student services leadership team has the mandate and natural role of serving as an advocate and catalyst for transformational change in response to the personal and academic needs of the diverse student body. This collegewide role may include the following dimensions:

- **Coordination and integration of services**. The student services leadership team can serve as the catalyst for coordinating and integrating student services across the divisions and programs.
- **Advocacy and institutional change.** The student services leadership team can serve as an advocate for collegewide responsiveness to the needs of the various groups of diverse students. The team seeks to bring about effective responses to individual student issues and promotes changes in policies, procedures, programs, services, and administrative practices.
- **Community development**. The student services leadership team can serve as a primary liaison with community agencies, organizations, and groups that serve populations who experience barriers to career and academic success. The team can also form college–community partnerships that enhance services to these populations.

Student Development or Student Flow Model

A *student development* or *student flow* model is based on the idea that each instructor and staff member directly or indirectly contributes to the development and success of students. At each stage of the student's journey from admissions to graduation, various departments and offices interact with students for good or for ill. Suppose, for example, that an Arab American student interprets a comment by a secretary, custodian, instructor, or staff member as discriminatory and stereotypic. Such a comment at any stage along the student's path through the college is hurtful and discouraging, and it damages the college's efforts to create an inclusive environment.

Suppose, on the other hand, that this instructor or staff member instead reaches out in a helpful and caring way to the Arab American student. In this case, both the student's self-concept and the college's image of inclusiveness are enhanced. Thus, the success of the student development model depends on the behavior and actions of all instructors and staff members as they interact with and serve students at each stage of development. In summary, the flow of student services can be outlined as follows:

- Building community relationships with families, schools, neighborhood groups, business organizations, and community groups from which potential students will come.
- Preadmissions, student marketing and recruitment, and enrollment management.
- Admissions, orientation, financial aid, assessment and testing, and academic advising.
- Registration, drop and add, and class placement.
- Counseling and student support: early alert programs, student skills services,

counseling and mental health services, special services, student activities, learning communities, support and self-help groups, etc.

- Pregraduation: graduation, career counseling, job placement, and university transfer services.
- Student follow-up: exit interviews, graduate follow-up, etc.

Table 8.2 Performance Indicators and Measurements for Assessing Student Services	
Indicator	**Measurement**
Student diversity	How closely enrollment reflects the demographics of the geographic service area
Penetration	Percentage of the population of the service area that is enrolled
Affordability	Percentage of students receiving financial aid, and tuition and fee rates as compared to other community colleges
Location	Convenience of service centers and online student services
Use of services	Number and percentage of students using counseling, special-needs services, and other student services
Student engagement	Number and percentage of students involved in out-of-class learning experiences; student clubs; multicultural, diversity, and equity activities; and community service
Student retention	Percentage of fall semester students who reenroll for the winter semester; percentage of students who reenroll from fall to fall
Student satisfaction	Percentage of students satisfied with each student service
Student goal attainment	Percentage of students who indicate that they achieved the goal for which they enrolled
Professional development of the student services staff	Percentage and scope of the professional development activities of the student services staff
Financial support of student services	Percentage of the college's operating budget that is allocated to student services compared with that of other community colleges

Emphasis on Effective Student Services

Measuring the effectiveness of student services is important in any case, but especially so when dramatic changes in student profiles are taking place. In addition, the assessment of the effectiveness, the documentation of performance evidence, and the documentation of service improvements made on the basis of the assessment data are basic requirements of regional accreditation bodies and federal government agencies. Are the services provided actually producing the outcomes that were intended in the lives of the students served? Are the outcomes data being used as a basis for identifying and implementing service improvements? Table 8.2 lists examples of general performance indicators that can guide the assessment of the effectiveness of student services.

BEST PRACTICES IN STUDENT SERVICES INNOVATION

Milwaukee Area Technical College

As one of the Midwest's largest community-based technical colleges, the Milwaukee Area Technical College offers 200 degree, diploma, certificate, and apprentice programs. With the most diverse student population of any college in Wisconsin, the Milwaukee Area Technical College has more than 57,000 students. The student services unit began its reengineering process by assembling a team of representatives from the college community. The transformation team reviewed processes and responded with a number of recommendations for personnel, environment, and technology. Its first strategy was to develop a customer-service training program and a related set of professional guidelines for instructors and staff. It also initiated a new call center and a series of improved practices and procedures.

Kirkwood Community College

Located in Cedar Rapids, Iowa, Kirkwood Community College has more than 15,000 credit students and 65,000 continuing education students served through 11 college centers and online instruction. Recognizing that a growing population of distance learners required support services, Kirkwood's transformation focused on how it was delivering services to its online students. Funded by a federal grant, it assembled a team of representatives from throughout the college who launched Support Online. The first task was to survey online learners to determine their specific needs. That was followed by a plan that identified three courses that used the services of a tutor, a supplemental instructor, and an advisor. This initial collaboration between student services and education affairs was successful, and it resulted in a plan to use this approach for other online classes.

Community College of Denver

The Community College of Denver has gained national recognition for its developmental education and student retention programs. Approximately 60% of its students are enrolled in developmental education classes. Administrators attribute the success of its efforts to an innovative, interdisciplinary approach to college support. Instructors are given time to tutor students in an individualized learning lab, and all students are required to attend a weekly session. In addition, the administration has assigned one department to oversee all operations related to developmental education.

Chaffey College

Chaffey College (California) is a 2-year community college that in 2003 received the Exemplary Program Award from the Board of Governors in the state of California for its basic skills transformation project—a 5-year program to bring about systemic change in the learning of basic literacy skills. Addressing the project from a strategic perspective, Chaffey College refocused its budgets, facilities, and organizational structure and changed its assessment processes, curriculum, instructional methods, academic support services, and staff professional development.

———

Community college student services leaders are transforming services in response to the varied personal and academic needs of diverse students. In addition to reinventing student services operations, they are moving student services toward a central, strategic, and collaborative role within the college. Based on traditional student services values of demonstrating a caring concern for each student and a commitment to equality, they are now advocates for change in collegewide policies, structures, and practices. They are serving as catalysts for integrating and coordinating student services with other college functions and programs. Student services divisions that were previously marginalized are being transformed to become primary agents for student access, student success, campuswide inclusiveness, and community engagement.

REFERENCES

Gibran, K. (1970). *The prophet.* New York: Knopf.

Chapter 9

Using Technology to Reach and Serve Diverse Students

Stephanie R. Bulger

Through the use of learning technologies, community colleges have become part of a global education community. Electronic modalities and telecommunications, which once encompassed online learning, videoconferencing, Internet access, and e-mail, have expanded and integrated into all instructional and support services offered by 2-year colleges. By incorporating them, community colleges have significantly expanded their community outreach, making the college experience accessible to many for whom on-campus, face-to-face services are not possible or not the best option. In addition to providing remote and off-campus accessibilities, these technologies have substantially enhanced on-campus instruction and student services by making on-demand learning resources available to students, instructors, advisors, and tutors. For example, digital libraries and online advisement and registration provide enhanced services to those with time constraints.

Distance learning brought the classroom in closer proximity to the student, using remote sites, including off-campus community college sites (also known as satellite centers), high schools, and other local or global venues to deliver instruction. Through distance learning, community colleges have played a major role in educating the diverse community college student body, which includes traditional and nontraditional students. One may think at first of the millennials, or Generation Y—those born in the United States and Canada during the 1980s and 1990s who naturally embrace various learning and networking technologies (Taylor, 2005). But many other constituencies are also affected, such as students living in other countries, those in the armed forces, students who are homebound due to physical disabilities or other factors, homemakers with small children, workplace learners, frequent travelers, and high school students who take community college classes electronically at home or at school. This technology has allowed education to enter the most remote sector of the population by availing itself to those who are incarcerated.

Community colleges from coast to coast are expanding their distance learning services to these emerging constituencies. Rio Salado College (Maricopa Community College District, Arizona), for example, has distance learning students in 130 countries and serves 1,500 military personnel posted around the world. With over 22,000 students enrolled in its more than 300 distance learning classes, it is a testament to the appeal and success of this technology. Wayne County Community College District (WCCCD) has developed a partnership with the Eritrean Institute of Technology in East Africa to provide distance learning to Institute students, and WCCCD's Virtual Middle College makes online college courses available to students from area high schools.

In this chapter, I address the ways in which community colleges can use technology to help students achieve their career and academic goals. I provide an overview of how technology and distance learning are changing academic course and program delivery, developmental education, and student services. I include current best practices for the use of technology in community colleges and explore the effect of these changes on costs and mission alignment. I also explore the challenges of the digital divide—the gap between the student's ability to utilize new and innovative technologies and the obstacles community colleges face in delivering them.

TECHNOLOGY APPEALS TO TODAY'S STUDENTS

Technological advances have allowed higher education to create options and services that are not bound by place and time. In turn, on-demand education has revolutionized the way that people learn and their desire for flexibility in the process. Technology has changed the ways in which information and services are delivered while helping educators to build relationships with their communities. Distance learning has expanded a community college's service area to the world. Data show that the yearning for on-demand education is unwavering. According to the last annual Instructional Technology Council (2008) survey of 154 community colleges, 70% reported that student demand exceeds the number of distance education courses offered. Administrators reported that instructor training and support for students who might have unrealistic expectations or limited technical skills are among their greatest challenges.

According to a survey of 2- and 4-year institutions (more than 2,500 total), more than 3.9 million students were enrolled in one or more online courses in fall 2007 (Allen & Seaman, 2008). That figure represents more than 20% of students enrolled in postsecondary education. Furthermore, nearly half of the 328,000 K–12 students took distance learning courses from a postsecondary school in 2005, and

78% of school districts expect to expand distance education offerings (Picciano & Seaman, 2007). From 2006 to 2007, online enrollment rose 12.9%, a rate of growth that surpassed the increase in enrollment. However, the proportion of colleges and universities that included online education as a critical component of their long-term strategy suffered a slight decline (Allen & Seaman, 2008).

In the face of competition from a number of public and private distance learning providers, community college leaders are well advised to understand, develop, and implement proactive strategies to reach and serve constituencies through distance learning. Providers such as online colleges, higher education online consortia, corporate universities, and international partnerships flourish, yet the largest numbers of students in online courses remain enrolled at 2-year institutions. According to CDW-G (2008), 94% of community colleges offer distance learning courses, compared with 74% of 4-year colleges and universities.

TECHNOLOGY FOR POSTSECONDARY EDUCATION

As the use of technologies such as mobile phones, video games, and the Internet has proliferated, students have come to expect to use technology in their education. Community colleges and others have responded by incorporating technology into traditional classrooms, smart classrooms, and virtual classroom environments. Course management systems are increasingly used in Web-assisted courses for asynchronous and synchronous online courses to allow instructors to create and share information while students can convene outside the classroom and locate support services from virtually anywhere off campus.

The new technologies being adopted for education further facilitate problem solving, collaboration, engagement, and social networking. Dubbed "next-generation teaching technologies" (Panettieri, 2007, p. 27), multi-user virtual environments and three-dimensional environments allow a person to control an avatar, a digitized representation of oneself in a simulated virtual environment. Telepresence, or enhanced digital video, lets viewers observe authentic representations of people in life-size forms and engage in realistic interactions with one another, regardless of their physical locations. Open-source content, which refers to the software, documents, and operating systems that have few intellectual property restrictions, offers greater flexibility, control, and low-cost or free access and use (see Voyles, 2007). Software applications for mobile technologies such as cell phones and iPod devices allow for wireless access to information that is untethered to the Internet. Location-aware services are applications that deliver location-based information, such as the locations of the bookstore and campus buildings, on demand (O'Hanlon, 2007). Savvy users are using social networking Web sites (e.g., MySpace and Facebook) and Web 2.0 technologies such as wikis and blogs to easily create and share information through text, audio, and video within online courses.

Clicker devices enable students to immediately respond to questions and classroom scenarios, giving instructors instant feedback on their teaching methods and the students' levels of comprehension. This technology also encourages participation and engagement by affording students the opportunity to interact individually and as a group. Other benefits of using clicker technology in the classroom are increases in attendance, preparation, discussion, and conceptual thinking (see, e.g., University of Tennessee Knoxville, 2009).

Online audio and video have found favor in college classes, both online and in the physical campus classroom. Youtube.com, a Web site for sharing digital video and audio files, has become a resource for hundreds of colleges, giving instructors and students an opportunity to upload video or audio presentations for use in the classroom and at home. Approximately 300 universities and colleges have their own channels on YouTube.edu, a segment of YouTube.com that is dedicated solely to secondary and postsecondary instruction and education (see, e.g., Bonk, 2009).

Simulated testing, artificial intelligence tutoring, and online assessment testing are strategic technologies that enhance instruction, increase retention, and improve critical thinking skills. Postsecondary institutions use them to assess knowledge, prepare students for higher-level certification and testing, and provide students with real-life applications relevant to course instruction. A study of 235 science majors at Duquesne University in Pennsylvania (Renshaw, 2005) showed a 45% increase in correct answers to questions after use of artificial tutoring and simulation tests. Similar simulated testing is widely used in community colleges to help students prepare for tests such as the ACT or ASLAT or certification examinations such as NCLEX.

Web Sites on Technology Use in Education

- Educause—www.educause.edu
- Instructional Technology Council—http://www.itcnetwork.org
- League for Innovation in the Community College and Project SAIL—www.league.org
- International Association for K–12 Online Learning—www.nacol.org http://www.inacol.org
- National University Telecommunications Network—www.nutn.org
- Sloan-C Consortium—www.sloan-c.org
- United States Distance Learning Association—www.usdla.org
- Western Cooperative for Educational Telecommunications—www.wcet.info/2.0/

Game-based learning has also revealed that students who are experienced video game players effectively adapt their skills to course content and learning. In 2006, game-based learning was a $125 million industry; however, there was no verification of its effectiveness. Three studies conducted at various universities revealed that business students who used game-based learning retained more interest and significantly higher means in score percentiles than did students who received the same instruction without game-based learning. The only variance was related to age—students under the age of 40 were more successful using game-based learning than were students 41 years of age and older (see Blunt, 2007). All of the foregoing examples demonstrate that advancing technology will serve as the driving force for changes in postsecondary education well into the foreseeable future.

TECHNOLOGY AND CHANGE IN THE COMMUNITY COLLEGE CURRICULUM

What we know from brain research and established theory about learning, particularly for adults, adds relevant information to our understanding of ways to adapt curricula for diverse students. Adult learning concepts and strategies for engagement are important in helping educators understand the unique characteristics of these learners (Conner, 1995). This understanding is especially important in the case of online learning because some of the support structures associated with traditional classroom instruction must be recreated in a new form for the remote learner. Knowles' (1984) principles are well known in adult learning circles. He provided a specific framework for understanding andragogy, the art and science of adult learning. He asserted that the following principles must be present for positive and effective adult learning environments:

- Learning environments are effective when they are safe places for learners.
- Active participation is crucial to the educational process.
- Real-life problems provide the stage for understanding and problem solving.
- New learning situations should be connected to current knowledge and experience.
- Learners should be guided to be self-directive in their learning.
- Opportunities for practice and constructive feedback must be provided.
- Time for reflection, analysis, and self-assessment of performance must be provided.

Similarly, Chickering and Gamson's 1987 research offered a concise view of quality teaching and learning practices in higher education. Their publication, *Seven Principles of Good Practice in Undergraduate Education,* has been widely used to inform discussions on undergraduate education. Although more than 20 years have passed since this document's publication, these principles apply to curricula and the quality of instructional design even today (cited in Sorcinelli, 1991). The principles are as follows:

- encouraging student–instructor contact
- encouraging cooperation among students
- encouraging active learning
- providing prompt feedback
- emphasizing time on task
- communicating high expectations
- respecting diverse talents and ways of learning

Ertmer and Newby (1993) have focused on applying strategy to curriculum design and asserted that the instructional approach used for novice learners might not be efficiently stimulating for a learner who is familiar with course concepts. They do not advocate one single learning theory but stress that instructional strategy and content depend on the level of the learners. They recommend matching learning theories with content objectives using a behavioral approach that can effectively facilitate mastery of the content of an area of study or profession (knowing what); cognitive strategies that can provide students with a set of problem-solving rules and strategies that can be used and applied to understand defined facts or process information in new and unfamiliar situations (knowing how); and constructivist strategies that are especially suited to dealing with ill-defined problems through reflection in action (Ertmer & Newby, 1993).

Effective learning design for adults requires relevance; connection to personal knowledge and experiences; and opportunities for interaction, practice, feedback, reflection, and personalization. The learning design creates conditions and situations that engage, stimulate, and motivate the student to participate in his or her own learning experiences. The strategies and principles described here provide a context for a discussion about the changing nature of curricula when applying use of technology. In online learning, technological tools such as interactive software, discussion boards, podcasts, audio and video sharing, social networking, group work, MySpace, Facebook, webcams, wikis, blogs, text and instant messaging, online portfolios, and synchronous online class sessions are practical applications of these learning principles and theories.

EXAMPLE OF COURSE REDESIGN USING INFORMATION TECHNOLOGY

The Program in Course Redesign conducted by the National Center for Academic Transformation is a notable project involving the effect of technology on curriculum change (Graves & Twigg, 2006). Launched in 1999, the program has collected nearly

10 years of data from 30 colleges and universities, including three community colleges. The purpose of this project was to demonstrate how instructional approaches can be redesigned by using technology to achieve quality and save money. About 25 courses generate approximately half of all student enrollments in community colleges. These courses include English, mathematics, psychology, sociology, economics, accounting, biology, and chemistry (Twigg, 2005a). The project focused on introductory courses because they exhibit a dropout, withdrawal, or failure rate of 50% or more in community colleges. The project identified the following five principles of successful course redesign efforts:

- Redesign the entire course as opposed to one section.
- Foster active learning in students.
- Give students personalized assistance.
- Provide assessment and immediate feedback throughout the course.
- Design the course for adequate time on task and frequent monitoring of student progress (Twigg, 2005a, pp. 1–10).

The Program on Course Redesign had a positive effect on the success of adult learners, minority students, and low-income students at Riverside Community College (California), Tallahassee Community College (Florida), and Rio Salado College (Arizona). At Riverside, students in redesigned math courses had substantially higher scores than did traditional students in four of six content areas on a common final exam. At Tallahassee, students in the redesigned composition course scored substantially higher on final essays than did students in the traditional course, regardless of ethnicity, gender, disability, or original placement. The overall success rate for all composition students was 62% for the 2002–2003 year compared with 56% for the 1999–2000 year, before the redesign. Rio Salado College increased retention rates from 59% to 64.8% in four of its online introductory math courses (Twigg, 2005b).

These community colleges combined several methods to engage students and increase their performance: required participation in on-demand assistance, required weekly class meetings, an early intervention system that identified students who were having difficulty, and creation of student learning teams within the larger course structure. The Program on Course Redesign project illustrates the value and necessity of continued contact with students, either by mandatory participation or by weekly class meetings, group work, and early interventions that identify and assist students who are at risk of dropping out, withdrawing, or failing. For more information regarding the Program on Course Redesign, see the Web site of the National Center for Academic Transformation (http://www.thencat.org/PCR.htm).

New technologies are being used to redesign courses, enabling institutions to create environments that address the learning modalities of today's computer-literate students. These technologies introduce exciting and varied teaching techniques and electronic learning capabilities. Document cameras allow instructors to capture and display 3-D images in real time, enhancing student comprehension, and SMART Board technology, podcasts, online accessibility, and file transfers have accelerated teaching and mastery of course objectives.

Since 2002, the *Horizon Report,* released by New Media Consortium and Educause, has identified emerging technologies slated to play a strategic and determinative role in postsecondary education in the future. The 2009 report identifies five technologies that will have a significant impact on the community college learning environment in the next 5 years (Johnson, Levine, & Smith, 2009).

- **Mobile technology.** Devices like the iPhone and the Blackberry have transformed communication devices from telephones to data centers. Tapping into their many capabilities, community college instructors and students can take advantage of their amenities, including graphic calculating, Internet and electronic communication, research, GPS functionality, and their ability to cross over many mediums and instantly access and relay information and data.
- **Cloud computing.** Through cloud computing, community colleges can outsource their computing needs to a virtual or independent entity, enhancing the public's access.
- **Geotagging.** This technology is used for enhancing photos, Web sites, videos, and other instructional media with geographical data identifiers.
- **Semantic-aware applications.** This technology interprets the meaning of information and finds relevant data on the Internet to develop solutions, accelerating traditional research, reasoning, and problem solving.
- **Smart objects.** These are ordinary objects that respond according to their physical location.

To date, technologies such as these have redesigned traditional course instruction. While some colleges and instructors utilize these technologies to supplement their traditional course outlines and delivery, others have identified areas in which technologies play a major role in instruction. Among those is the use of smart technology, which has a substantial impact not only on the way information is delivered to the student, but also on the environment in which it is received. Active learning centers that implement smart technologies incorporate tools like mobile furniture, document cameras, interactive whiteboards, and individual huddleboards—tools that display information and encourage discussion, participation, and collaboration among students.

Another way in which technology is redesigning the traditional classroom is that it eliminates the time-consuming need for note-taking, which often impairs students' abilities to listen and comprehend the material that is being presented. The capability of wireless tablets to store and download classroom lectures frees students from the task of taking laborious notes, giving them the opportunity to pen questions while the information is presented, making both the question and the answer accessible to the class as a cohesive unit.

TECHNOLOGY IN DEVELOPMENTAL EDUCATION

Technology is affecting developmental education in unexpected ways. There is a common notion that developmental students lack the skills to succeed in courses using technology. Indeed, the Instructional Technology Council's 2008 survey showed that students' lack of technology skills is one of their greatest challenges. However, there is another view: For many developmental students, using technology affords them a new beginning to learn a skill or concept, (see, e.g., McCabe, 2003). The research that supports this view suggests the need for greater support services and more time on task for students to develop technology skills.

In addition, developmental students benefit from the variety of instruction received through innovation and technology. For instance, students with hearing impairments who are enrolled in classes that use clicker technologies with visual screens to answer multiple choice and true/false questions are afforded an opportunity to interact with the rest of the class and the instructor in real time. These technologies allow developmental students to integrate into the student body and classroom at higher levels than in learning environments and with methods that rely solely on lecture.

Wireless tables and other smart technologies have enhanced learning for those with language barriers. Students who are uncomfortable speaking or unable to speak in class or ask questions welcome the anonymity of writing or typing thoughts, answers, and questions through various computer technologies. Voice annotation software enhances this technology even further.

In a study of nine community colleges and 2,381 students taking courses in English, math, and ESL, researchers examined the effectiveness of instructional approaches using computer technology for developmental students (Johnson, 2000). This study revealed five major approaches that produced success, as well as persistence, in this population: (1) providing an orientation on computer lab policies, available assistance, and software usage; (2) developing adequate typing skills by midterm; (3) allowing sufficient time for people with weak computer skills to gain proficiency; (4) matching the course objectives to activities in the software; and (5) coaching the instructional tutor to have multiple functions, such as tutor, trainer, and problem solver. These steps served as the building blocks to students' academic success.

Another study addressed attitudes and perceptions held by education support organizations that serve low-income adults about online postsecondary education (Benson, 2007). Results of this qualitative study showed that organizations that were successful in serving low-income adults taking online courses had four common elements:

- They expected students to be successful in online learning despite their lack of experience with computers.
- They referred students who needed additional computer training to sources that could provide it.
- They were sensitive to the unique and diverse learning needs of adults and

provided them with tutoring assistance.

- There was frequent communication between the colleges and education support organizations on ways to support the adults.

Results across the board indicate that developmental students benefit from the use of technology in the classroom because it provides flexibility, reduces seat time, increases computer literacy that greatly enhances their ability to succeed in upper-level courses, and offers them access to help and tutoring when they need it.

TECHNOLOGY IN STUDENT SERVICES

It is easy to comprehend that curriculum change can have a major effect on student learning. Less apparent is the way that technology can be used to provide supportive services to students who are not physically present on campus. For the past several decades, student services professionals have used technology to serve students in a variety of ways, as well as for administrative functions such as records management. Current drivers of changes to student services include students' interest in convenience, global access to greater options for higher education, a heightened marketing emphasis on recruitment and customer service, and the focus on learning outcomes by national accreditation associations. For instance, a review of the accreditation criteria by the Higher Learning Commission of the North Central Association of Colleges and Schools shows a focus on demonstrating student outcomes in student services as opposed to simply accounting for services. Core component 3c, for example, says that "The organization creates effective learning environments…[if] advising systems focus on student learning, including the mastery of skills required for academic success" (Higher Learning Commission, 2003, p. 3.1–4). As student services functions migrate from traditional processing functions to a focus on student development, learning outcomes, and learning environments, technology could be used to serve the needs of students in the following ways, as identified by Cross (2000):

- Informing students about courses, programs, registration processes, and the like in kiosks, on CD-ROM, on the college's YouTube channel, and on the college's Web site.
- Providing several ways to enroll and pay—online, by telephone, and in person.
- Assessing capabilities and challenges, including online placement testing as well as aptitude and personality tests.
- Advising students in several ways, such as online and in person.
- Supporting students through online orientation, online tutoring, and early warning systems for those in academic trouble.
- Connecting students to one another through communications and networking technologies.

- Providing interactive software for financial aid and scholarship applications.
- Making disability support services available online.
- Providing up-to-date information on student groups, activities, and meetings.
- Assisting students with career placement by providing online job applications and assistance with filling out applications and writing resumés.
- Assisting in students' transitions to careers or 4-year universities by using technology for portfolio management, job openings, and university degree transfer information.

No matter their preparation level, today's community college students have high expectations for customer service and convenience. They expect that convenient learning, communications, and networking technologies will be available to them, just as they are in workplaces, coffee houses, banks, airports, community libraries, hotels, and most of their homes. There are many ways in which community colleges can respond to these student demands, including the following:

- Expand the availability of on-campus computing resources by increasing the number of computer labs available and creating schedules for on-campus labs that accommodate early morning and late-night use.
- Make staff available for personalized assistance and service.
- Make bandwidth requirements and accommodations available to students who use outside computers to access course material from home or work. For example, instructions for optimizing course-related audio and video files as well as downloads for those players could be available to students on college Web sites.
- Increase the number of courses that encourage online homework submission, allowing the students' scores to be calculated electronically and made available for review immediately.
- Increase Web site services such as credit card payments, admissions, degree audit software, and digital music services (see Following the Web 2.0 Piper, 2007; McClure, 2007).
- Be prepared for the next generation of technologies for managing the student's relationship with the college (called *student life-cycle management*) that tracks the student through recruitment, admissions, retention, graduation, and beyond (see Villano, 2007, pp. 41–42).

ORGANIZATIONAL IMPACTS OF TECHNOLOGY

Costs of Instruction

There is evidence that technology can be used to reduce the costs of instruction. The Program in Course Redesign project offers the following suggestions:

- Use online tutorials that are Web-based or on DVD, CD-ROM, or flash drives.
- Reduce lecture time to focus on the difficult concepts experienced by students.
- Automate exercises, quizzes, and tests that students can practice without an instructor.
- Use lower-cost staff, such as course assistants, rather than higher-cost instructors, to help students with technology and administrative tasks.
- Share resources among instructors by creating materials that eliminate duplicated efforts in designing course materials.
- To save instructors time, use course management systems for conducting routine tasks such as grading homework and examinations.
- Reduce classroom space needs by using Web content and course management systems for class instruction.
- Consolidate sections and courses into large sections taught in a computer lab.

The institutions involved in the Program in Course Redesign project used technology-based approaches and learner-centered principles to redesign their courses without sacrificing cost or quality. By beginning with learning outcomes, these institutions avoided traditional thinking and designed effective and efficient learning environments (Twigg, 2003). Evaluating possible cost savings by using technology to create efficiencies while enhancing student learning must be weighed against the investments that will surely need to be made to provide technology for curriculum revisions, development, and student services. Moreover, the costs of upgrades to computer hardware, software, servers, and technical support must be considered necessary ancillaries of this investment by community colleges.

In planning technological advances in the community college environment, administrators can rely on Moore's law, which has defined the future ability and costs of computer technologies for 40 years. According to Moore's law, every 2 years the capacity of microchips will double, while their size will be reduced by one half. Furthermore, as technology increases every 2 years, the cost to the user will be reduced by 50%. Also taking into account Metcalfe's law, which states that the value of a network is in direct correlation to it size, one can see the various components that should be considered when determining the value of instructional and support costs to integrate technology.

Community colleges and other public education institutions must plan for and request new equipment and staff as much as one year in advance. Approximately 60% of a community college's funding comes from government agencies, which limits capabilities and the acquisition of the newest and most advanced technologies. In planning future technological changes, community college administrators will need to review state funding practices, operational guidelines, strategic priorities, and state funding formulas for the appropriation of allocations. Insofar as capital projects, strong attention to meeting expectations for growth of student enrollment and capacity load and for reducing the costs of projects will be required.

As community colleges meet the increase in student demand that often results from a suffering economy, they must also rely heavily on strategic planning to overcome the challenges ahead of them and meet the needs of their student bodies and communities. Given the financial constraints imposed on community colleges in the present economy, community college administrators and planners must place greater importance on the technological advances that will be the least costly and more likely to affect the greatest number of students, courses, support services, and community needs.

When assessing how technology and online course availability affects a college's financial resources, Metcalfe's law comes into play. Community colleges have traditionally focused their costs on classroom seat availability (i.e., the more seats filled, the more fiscally viable the course). However, online learning and distance learning have turned that modality upside down by creating virtual, rather than physical, seats. Thus, financial feasibility will also grow with the number of students enrolled in each section, and the value of the online learning community will increase in direct relation to its size.

The challenges to community colleges across the country in increasing the availability of technology and accessibility to remote learning and resources are in funding, planning, and staffing. These limitations require creative thinking and long-term research and planning to identify technologies that not only can be funded, but also that will actually reduce the cost of instruction per student over time. One writer on technology and the community college encouraged community colleges to be "resourceful, resilient, and ready" (Ramaswami, 2009). Some colleges have successfully found the means to increase their technological capabilities and accessibility while actually reducing overhead expenditures for equipment and labor. Virtual servers and data processors and computer-driven alternatives to traditional tasks have reduced costs at some colleges.

The cost of instruction is one of the largest budget appropriations for community colleges. While technology can reduce the amount of actual instruction time spent in the classroom, it can increase the number of preparation and office hours. Distance learning and online courses require extensive development by program coordinators and full-time instructors. They also affect the number of office hours required for the instructors responsible for them. In the community college environment, a specific formula is often used to determine the number of classroom hours and the number of office hours that instructors must incorporate into their schedules. Contract negotiations and union demands weigh heavily on those formulas.

Traditionally, however, instructors were required to have 1 hour of office time for every 2 hours of lecture in the classroom, with a percentage reduction for classroom lab hours. Distance learning and online learning must equate into the formula, while unions have requested class-size limitations for online instructors. These limitations reduce the impact of the additional seats created in a virtual learning environment. To offset those costs, community colleges can seek adjunct or part-time instructors for distance learning courses. In addition, institutions that increase the roles of IT and support staff and those that take advantage of the knowledge and expertise of lab assistants and student aides as less expensive alternates and enhancements to instruction can deliver quality content at a lesser price.

Use of technology in teaching and learning will effect changes in upper administration and in the traditional manner of managing seat time and graduation requirements. The traditional Carnegie unit recognized that student competency was synonymous with seat time and awarded students with credit hours based on time spent in the classroom. The Carnegie unit—the credit hour—used to measure classroom hours in 120 sixty-minute segments, was developed in 1906 and became a model for secondary and postsecondary academic evaluation and achievement (Shedd, 2003). Distance and online learning cannot measure seat time and must, therefore, evaluate competency based on other standards, incorporating demonstration, assessment, and comprehension of course objectives and their applications. Using this model, students can effectively demonstrate their competency and successful course completion in less time than they would by physically attending traditional classrooms.

As technology reduces the relevance of the Carnegie unit, however, it is also likely to increase student retention, success, and graduation rates. Community colleges with high levels of retention and graduation and low levels of withdrawals, failures, and dropouts merit the benefits of accreditation and are more likely to receive grants and capital appropriations to further their outreach and impact on the communities they serve. As microtechnology, macrotechnology, and creative innovation grows, the levels of student satisfaction and success seen thus far are likely to grow, making technology the mainstay of the community college rather than a component of it.

So, by advancing technology within the community college, the institution is afforded the opportunity to increase student success and accelerate program or degree completion. In return, institutions will receive a higher return on their technological investments by increasing the availability of seats (which traditionally measured the financial feasibility of course offerings) and the number of students paying tuition and fees. These increases will offset the costs of obtaining technology and the in-house staffing needs to maintain it.

According to the 2009 national trends report by the State Educational Technology Directors Association, secondary schools that integrate technology in course content, instruction, assessments, and professional development have a higher level of academic achievement, a 14% increase in graduation rates, and students who are better prepared for the college environment (see also Nagel, 2009). Similar results are being sought at the community college level. The American Graduation Initiative (AGI) focuses on the efforts of community colleges to increase the number of graduates who have the skills and education to meet the future demands of a changing workforce. Among the program's goals is increasing the number of community college graduates by 5 million students by the year 2020. Technology is a mainstay in the initiative, which aims to provide grant funding, nontraditional program or certificate completion methods, and the modernization of college facilities and equipment. Perhaps the most supportive technological component of this initiative is the creation of an online skills laboratory or online repository. This online repository will utilize and expand the concepts of online courses, data, research, simulations, and testing. Interactive software will be specially designed to meet this purpose, providing tailored instruction based on an individual's needs and goals. Ultimately, AGI will also address the challenge of awarding academic credit based on achievement (see White House, 2009).

Recruitment and Development of Instructors

As community college leaders consider the costs of restructuring the academic curriculum and student services to incorporate technology in ways that meet the learning needs and desires of diverse students, they must also consider the recruitment and development of instructors. Several factors have influenced the need to reconsider approaches to recruitment and development. First, in the case of online course and program development, a collaborative approach often works best. Instructors might not be the sole designers but might be co-creators in the curriculum development process. Instructors, instructional designers, and multimedia specialists might be members of a program development team.

Second, the number of instructors trained to teach using technology constitutes a small part of the whole. Instructor recruits can be quickly exhausted in a given college community. Strategies for developing new instructors with skills in using technology and teaching distance learning courses might need to expand beyond the typical advertisement in the local newspaper and periodic recruitment events. Third, instructors who teach online or via videoconferencing require special training and should be able to demonstrate that they are prepared to teach in these modalities. Standards of quality should be available to instructors, and training strategies should also be developed.

Fourth, today's students communicate by e-mail and mobile devices. In-person office hours are less critical for them, as is immediate or reasonable access to their instructors within, say, 24 hours. Fifth, traditional instructor hiring processes involve an evaluation of credentials for the appropriate education and experience, and they might include a demonstration component of a lecture. Today's hiring requirements might also include an evaluation of an instructor's use of technology to encourage higher levels of participation in students in multiple arenas (e.g., the face-to-face classroom, online, videoconferencing, and smart classrooms).

One strategy is to develop in-house training for online instructors. Online teaching uses different and new pedagogies. Therefore, it requires a process that assesses the candidate's current skills and experience using technology, as well as a comprehensive development and training program. As an example, in 2004, WCCCD established a certification program that was designed to help instructors build technological skills and understand how to effectively incorporate these skills into their online pedagogical and classroom management practices. This program has three parts:

- **Blackboard basics.** This 4-hour in-person workshop covering the tools in Blackboard, a proprietary online course management system, concludes with an assessment, during which instructors demonstrate their proficiency in using Blackboard tools. Instructors might need to retake this assessment before completing their training to teach online.
- **Pedagogy and online instructor training.** During this 3–week online experience facilitated by a trainer, instructors review principles of online course design, pedagogy, and classroom management. They complete assignments and meet deadlines, including constructing an online course in an environment that also simulates an online course.
- **Course shadowing.** During this 7-week experience, candidates for online instructor certification are paired with experienced online instructors. Candidates are required to complete and submit a weekly report on their experience.

A second strategy is to integrate external resources into a college's existing processes. One such effort is Quality Matters (www.qualitymatters.org), an organization that promotes a peer-review system designed to certify the quality of online courses by evaluating course design. Coordinated by a set of partner institutions and state consortia, this organization offers subscriptions that include training for course peer reviews.

A third strategy is to develop a college-sponsored, comprehensive organizational development program for instructors, administrators, and staff. What began as a series of workshops for midlevel administrators at WCCCD has evolved into a comprehensive Organizational Development Institute that is designed to increase skills, build culture, and support the college mission (WCCCD, 2009). Offered for 8 months of the academic year, the institute consists of five tracks—instruction, distance learning, banner training, managing and leading, and skills enrichment. The institute's workshops are enhanced by an orientation course, an annual district conference day, and an annual conference on great leadership.

Through these efforts, WCCCD seeks to support the district's "commitment to student success, community outreach and economic development" (WCCCD, 2008, p. 1). In addition, the district has a grow-your-own strategy that strives to prepare employees to assume additional responsibilities to meet the education needs of students, increased demands for financial accountability, and the need to demonstrate instructional quality, excellence, and successful education outcomes.

Given the costs associated with assigning additional courses to the load of full-time faculty members, community colleges can explore the viability of using adjunct or part-time instructors to meet the increased demand for instructors resulting from increased seat capacity. On the other hand, some argue that adjunct instructors do not provide the same high-level quality of instruction as do their full-time counterparts. An effective training and certification program for delivery of online instruction can answer those concerns by assigning instructors to oversee distance learning courses. Similarly, relevant and comprehensive student and faculty evaluations of those courses and their delivery will enable community colleges to ensure that they are delivering adequate quality and content in their remote courses and technological offerings.

ALIGNING TECHNOLOGY WITH MISSION AND STRATEGY

The use of technology holds the promise of powerful and positive effects on fulfilling the community college mission; however, community college leaders should consider developing strategic plans regarding the use of technology in instruction and services and to develop executable goals (see, e.g., McCabe, 2003). With the following strategies, suggested by Boettcher (2007), community colleges can begin to incorporate technology into their mission of access and success, community outreach, and support of the economic viability of their regions:

- Make online learning part of the community college organization, increasing the support of online learning programs and initiatives with administration, staff, and faculty and in the community it serves.
- Center online initiatives and efforts around the student body sector that needs online accessibility.
- Strive to adopt a top-down approach, meaning that the institution's leaders and administrators should be strong proponents for online education and distance learning. Their support will contribute greatly toward facilitating support from instructors, faculty, and the community. It will also benefit the college's budget planning and appropriations, giving the advancement of such technologies a higher priority within the institution.

THE DIGITAL DIVIDE

All the strategies offered thus far force us to recognize the assumption that students have access to technology and use it for education. Yet we know that this is not always the case. We recognize that there are students whose access to and use of technology is limited because of their socioeconomic status and other factors. Are students who are at risk because of factors such as low income and limited literacy skills on the losing end of the digital divide? It is clear that many students stand to become have-nots in the digital divide because many do not have access to computers in their homes even though they may have personal digital assistants and cell phones for personal and recreational purposes other than education or training.

If people are to compete politically, economically, and educationally in the 21st century, they must have access to and knowledge of computers and the Internet. The importance of computer access and use is emphasized by Thomas Friedman in *The World is Flat:*

> [T]he Indias and Chinas are increasingly adding one more thing to low-cost labor with high-power technology: unfettered imagination—that is, high innovative and creative capacities. They will focus first on solving their own problems with cheap labor, high technology, and high creativity—re-imagining their own futures. Then they will focus on ours. We must have people, lots of people, who can do the same. (2006, p. 390)

Evidence suggests that there is a persistent digital divide in the United States based on income, education, and race. For example, in an analysis of a representative sample of 50,000 U.S. households, Fairlie (2003) found that Hispanics, Blacks, and Native Americans who had low levels of education and income owned computers and used the Internet at home much less than Whites and Asian Americans did. Forty percent of Blacks and Hispanics and 20% of Whites reported that cost limited their ability to have the Internet at home. Blacks and Hispanics who made at least $60,000 were still less likely than Whites to have computers and Internet access at home, suggesting that there are additional explanations for the gaps (Fairlie, 2003). Some of these explanations were found in the differences between occupations held by the respondents—for example, low versus high levels of computer use outside the home. Language barriers also explained a small part of the gap between computer owners and Internet users.

Although the percentage of people who use the Internet is growing, disparities persist within race, class, education, and household income in the demographics of Internet users (Pew Internet, 2009; U.S. Department of Commerce, 2004). Even though students of different backgrounds might have varying levels of technological skill and access to resources, it is the responsibility of community colleges to provide equal access to all because technology is the cornerstone of education. Some may learn, use, and adapt to technology differently depending on the social, political, and technological environment of their youth and adulthood. For example, the conditions that support learning for baby boomers who grew up without most of the current technology is likely different from those of Generation X and millenials who were raised with widespread access to cell phones, iPods, high-speed Internet, and easily portable laptop computers (see Taylor, 2005).

As open-door colleges, community colleges have been responding to the challenges of the digital divide through innovations such as making laptop computers available for library checkout, including the cost of a computer in scholarship programs, expanding computer lab hours, and cooperating with community libraries and social services centers to create neighborhood computer labs. Communities that work together to bridge the digital divide might make the greatest strides to cross it (see www.onecommunity.org for an example).

━━━◦◦◦◦━━━

Community college students are more diverse and numerous than ever. They enroll with a unique set of needs that instructors and administrators must address to effectively serve them. Coupled with this challenge is the tremendous growth of online credit courses and degree programs in community colleges and the availability of more sophisticated technology. Community colleges have a unique opportunity to create environments that foster the use of appropriate technology to enhance learning and outcomes. A multifaceted approach is required to meet this imperative with strategic planning and investment in technology as well as ongoing training, support, and resources for all concerned. Although this process will be as long, complex, and difficult as the pace of technology itself, the result will be a new infrastructure to support a positive learning environment and success for diverse students who might otherwise be left behind. As *Futurist* author James Martin noted, "A tragedy of humankind today is that most people fall outrageously short of their potential. A goal of the twenty-first century ought to be to develop the capability latent in everybody by harnessing powerful technologies that accelerate learning potential" (Martin, 2007, p. 20).

REFERENCES

Allen, E., & Seaman, J. (2008, November). *Staying the course: Online education in the United States,* Needham, MA: Sloan Consortium. Retrieved from http://www.sloan-c.org/publications/survey/pdf/staying_the_course.pdf

Benson, A. D. (2007, Winter). An exploratory study of online postsecondary education for low-income working adults: A view from education support programs. *Journal of Negro Education 76*(1), 17. (ERIC # EJ770239)

Blunt, R. (2007). *Does game-based learning work? Results from three recent studies.* Retrieved from http://www.reality-xp.com/professional/files/GameBasedLearningStudies.pdf

Boettcher, J. V. (2007, February 1). Getting the money right. *Campus Technology,* 18–22. Retrieved from http://campustechnology.com/articles/2007/02/getting-the-money-right.aspx

Bonk, C. (2009, October). Using shared online video to anchor instruction: Youtube and beyond. *Instructional Design, Trends in Higher Education.* Retrieved from http://www.facultyfocus.com/articles/instructional-design/using-shared-online-video-to-anchor-instruction-youtube-and-beyond/

CDW-G. (2008, October). *The 21st-century campus: Are we there yet?* Retrieved from http://newsroom.cdwg.com/features/feature-10-13-08.html

Conner, M. (1995). *Learning: The critical technology: A whitepaper on adult education in the information age* (3rd ed.). St. Louis, MO: Wave Technologies International, Inc. Retrieved from http://learnativity.com/download/Learning_Whitepaper96.pdf

Cross, C. (2000). Cyber-counseling, virtual registration, and student self-service: Student services in the information age. In M. Milliron & C. Miles (Eds.), *Taking a big picture look @ technology, learning, and the community college* (pp. 157–159). Phoenix, AZ: League for Innovation in the Community College. (ERIC # ED447843)

Ertmer, P. A., & Newby, T. J. (1993). Behaviorism, cognitivism, and constructivism: Comparing critical features from a design perspective. *Performance Improvement Quarterly, (6)*4, 50–72.

Fairlie, R. W. (2003, November). *Is there a digital divide? Ethnic and racial differences in access to technology and possible explanations.* Retrieved from http://cjtc.ucsc.edu/docs/r_techreport5.pdf

Following the Web 2.0 Piper. (2007, February 1). *Campus technology.* Retrieved from http://www.campustechnology.com/Articles/2007/02/Following-the-Web-20-Piper.aspx

Friedman, T. L. (2006). *The world is flat: A brief history of the twenty-first century* (2nd ed.). New York: Farrar, Strauss, and Giroux.

Graves, W., & Twigg, C. (2006, February/March). The future of course redesign and the National Center for Academic Transformation: An interview with Carol A. Twigg. *Innovate Online, 2*(3). Retrieved from http://innovateonline.info/index.php?view=article&id=218&action=article

Higher Learning Commission. (2003). *Handbook of accreditation* (3rd ed.). Chicago: Author. Retrieved from http://www.ncahlc.org/download/Handbook03.pdf

Instructional Technology Council. (2008). *2007 distance education survey results: Tracking the impact of e-learning at community colleges.* Washington, DC: Author.

Johnson, L. F. (2000). Into the breach: A national study of computers and the "at risk." In M. Milliron & C. Miles (Eds.), *Taking a big picture look @ technology, learning, and the community college* (pp. 223–250). Phoenix, AZ: League for Innovation in the Community College. (ERIC # ED447843)

Johnson, L., Levine, A., & Smith, R. (2009). *The 2009 horizon report.* Austin, TX: The New Media Consortium.

Knowles, M. S. (1984). *Andragogy in action: Applying modern principles of adult learning.* San Francisco: Jossey-Bass.

Martin, J. (2007, January/February). The 17 great challenges of the twenty-first century. *The Futurist: Forecasts, Trends, and Ideas About the Future,* 20–24. Available from the World Future Society Web site: http://www.wfs.org

McCabe, R. H. (2003). *Yes we can! A community college guide for developing America's underprepared.* Washington, DC: Community College Press. (ERIC # ED475435)

McClure, A. (2007, March). It's electric: Colleges and universities are finding that an electronic admissions process can improve efficiency while still making students feel unique. *University Business.* Retrieved from http://www.universitybusiness.com/ViewArticle.aspx?articleid=701

Nagel, D. (2009, April 2). Study ties student achievement to technology integration. *The Journal: Transforming Education Through Technology.* Retrieved from http://thejournal.com/articles/2009/04/02/study-ties-student-achievement-to-technology-integration.aspx

O'Hanlon, C. (2007, February 1). Location-aware services: Where on earth…? *Campus Technology,* 33–44. Retrieved from http://www.campustechnology.com/Articles/2007/02/LocationAware-Services--Where-on-Earth.aspx

Panettieri, J. (2007, January). Advanced teaching technologies: Brave new world. *Campus Technology,* 27–33. Retrieved from http://campustechnology.com/Articles/2006/12/Advanced-Teaching-Technologies-Brave-New-World.aspx

Pew Internet & American Life Project. (2009, July 22). *Wireless Internet use.* Retrieved from http://www.pewinternet.org/Reports/2009/12-Wireless-Internet-Use.aspx

Picciano, A. G., & Seaman, J. (2007). K–12 online learning: A survey of U.S. school district administrators. *Journal of Asynchronous Learning Networks, 11*(3). Retrieved from http://www.sloanconsortium.org/publications/jaln/v11n3/v11n3_3piccianoseaman_member.asp

Ramaswami, R. (2009, March). Technology and the community college, the three R's: Resourceful, resilient, and ready. *Campus Technology.* Retrieved from http://campustechnology.com/articles/2009/03/01/technology-and-the-community-college.aspx

Renshaw, A. (2005, February). Duquesne University students improve problem-solving ability by 45% with Quantum artificial intelligence tutors. *Quantum Simulations.* Retrieved from http://www.quantumsimulations.com/news16.html

Shedd, J. (2003, Summer). The history of the student credit hour. In *New Directions for Higher Education, No. 122.* New York: Wiley.

Sorcinelli, M. D. (1991, Fall). Research findings on the seven principles. *New Directions for Teaching and Learning, 1991(47),* 13–25. (ERIC # EJ436070)

State Educational Technology Directors Association. (2009, March). *Focus on technology integration in America's schools.* Washington, DC: Author. Available at www.setda.org

Taylor, M. (2005). Generation next comes to college: 2006 updates and emerging issues. In S. Van Kollenburg (Ed.), *A collection of papers on self-study and institutional improvement. Vol. 2: Focusing on the needs and expectations of constituents* (pp. 2:48–2:55). Chicago: Higher Learning Commission of the North Central Association.

Twigg, C. (2003). Quality, cost, and access. In M. S. Pittinsky (Ed.), *The wired tower: Perspectives on the impact of the Internet on higher education* (pp. 111–143). Upper Saddle River, NJ: Prentice Hall.

Twigg, C. (2005a, June). *Course redesign improves learning and reduces cost.* San Jose, CA: The National Center for Public Policy and Higher Education. Retrieved from http://www.highereducation.org/reports/pa_core/core.pdf

Twigg, C. (2005b). *Program in course redesign: Rio Salado College.* Saratoga Springs, NY: National Center for Academic Transformation. Retrieved from http://www.thencat.org/PCR/R1/RSC/RSC_Overview.htm

U. S. Department of Commerce. (2004, September). *A nation online: Entering the broadband age.* Washington, DC: Author. Retrieved from http://www.ntia.doc.gov/reports/anol/index.html

University of Tennessee at Knoxville. (2009). *Technology changes at UT Knoxville.* Retrieved from http://itc.utk.edu/classrooms/clickers/

Villano, M. (2007, February 1). Student lifecycle management: CRM meets the campus. *Campus Technology.* Retrieved from http://campustechnology.com/articles/2007/02/student-lifecycle-management--crm-meets-the-campus.aspx

Voyles, B. (2007, February 1). Data mining and business intelligence: Open for business. *Campus Technology.* Retrieved from http://www.campustechnology.com/Articles/2007/02/Data-Mining—Business-Intelligence--Open-for-Business.aspx

Wayne County Community College District. (2009, Spring). *Organizational development institute: Reach your highest potential.* Retrieved from http://www.wcccd.edu/dept/pdf/ODI%20book%20complete.pdf

White House, Office of the Press Secretary. (2009, July). *American Graduation Initiative.* Retrieved from http://www.whitehouse.gov/the_press_office/Excerpts-of-the-Presidents-remarks-in-Warren-Michigan-and-fact-sheet-on-the-American-Graduation-Initiative/

Chapter 10

Meeting New Challenges and Demands for Workforce Education

James Jacobs

I f there is one common mission identified with community colleges, it is workforce education: the ability of these colleges to provide courses and programs that prepare students for work or for advancement within their present jobs. Some researchers view the workforce education mission as one of the primary roles of comprehensive community colleges, often to the detriment of other important missions such as transfer to 4-year colleges (Dougherty, 1992). Certainly, the identification of community colleges with workforce education is a view widely shared by the public. In 2004, a public relations firm commissioned a national survey of adults to determine their perceptions of community colleges. The overall view was extremely positive, with a consensus that the public sees community colleges as gateways to opportunity, institutions of higher education that could give people the skills to find work (Belden Russonello & Stewart, 2004).

Workforce education is a central mission that is assumed, accepted, and promoted among community college policymakers. The American Association of Community Colleges (AACC) views workforce and economic development as one of its five strategic action areas (AACC, 2006). Many community colleges identify workforce development as part of their mission statement. Changes in the U.S. workplace and in the students will challenge the success of these colleges in the area of workforce education. As the U.S. economy enters a new phase, dominated by globalization of production systems and computer-based technologies, many high-paying semiskilled jobs are being eliminated, resulting in substantial income inequalities and in employment only for those with degrees or advanced skills. At the same time, community colleges are attracting greater numbers of underprepared students who lack the skills to qualify for these jobs. The bar is being raised for colleges in both how they design workforce education programs and how they can elevate the skills of underprepared students to obtain this work. The new skill demands of the workplace and the changes in community college students pose considerable challenges to the ability of community colleges to execute their workforce education mission effectively.

THE EVOLUTION OF THE WORKFORCE EDUCATION MISSION

The community colleges' reputation in workforce education was honed in the post–World War II economic expansion. Although they were in existence for most of the 20th century, these 2-year junior colleges were previously concerned primarily with preparing students for transfer to 4-year colleges and for careers in broad occupational areas such as health care and business. After World War II, however, in an expanding economy dominated by large manufacturing and retail corporations, the level of employee skills needed by these large firms increased considerably. When companies such as General Motors, Boeing, and Sears expanded their production and technical activities, community colleges provided their semiskilled human resources.

The schools were also well positioned to respond to the vast expansion of jobs within the midlevel technical occupations. The introduction of computer applications to operate electronically controlled machinery resulted in the elimination of large numbers of unskilled workers and a proliferation of new jobs in the technical service and design functions associated with these processes. These occupations required more than high school but less than a 4-year degree. As these jobs increased, working adults had to upgrade their skills. Local community colleges thrived on the new enrollments and became more comprehensive by meeting the needs of incumbent workers for increased job skills (Cohen & Brawer, 2003).

Other semiskilled job growth occurred in white-collar occupations such as accounting, marketing, and data processing as more companies developed mainframe computer systems for payroll, human resources, and other activities. There was also a substantial increase in public-sector jobs for police, firefighters, and corrections officers, while other public service occupations were being professionalized at all levels.

Nursing may be the quintessential example of community colleges answering the increased demand for technical workers. Previously, nurses either received their training in hospital-based diploma programs or were trained in 4-year programs as professional nurses. As health-care facilities expanded, the demand for nurses far exceeded the ability of other programs to train them. Community colleges stepped in, and by the early 1980s, more than 60% of nurses in the United States came from associate degree programs (Karp, Jacobs, & Hughes, 2002).

From Junior College to Comprehensive Community College

The rapid and comprehensive expansion of career and technical programs transformed the 2-year junior college into a new college that served both transfer and career functions. Fueled in part by the federal Career and Technical Education Act of 1963 (renamed the Carl Perkins Vocational Education Act in 1984) and state and local concerns for economic development, enrollments in occupational courses grew. During this period, many colleges developed 1-year certificate programs in many occupational areas, concentrating on the technical skills needed for these occupations; these shorter programs became quite popular.

The expansion of the workforce education programs came to be seen as benefiting individuals and employers while contributing to local and state economic growth. These programs were highly promoted to public policymakers by community college leaders as a meaningful component of economic development. In the late 1980s, many states adopted business retention strategies that included making substantial training funds available to local industry through the community college system. New customized training units or business and industry units emerged on the campus alongside the traditional career and technical programs (Jacobs, 1989).

By the early 1990s, new changes in the workplace were again transforming the role of community colleges in workforce education. The majority of formal technical training for manufacturing firms was now being performed by community colleges. Policymakers developing new government workforce programs and needy family programs often assumed that community colleges would deliver the training in their systems (Jacobs, 2001). Even the former chairman of the Federal Reserve, Alan Greenspan, noted the contributions of community colleges in workforce preparation:

> One area in which educational investments appear to have paid off
> is our community colleges. These two-year institutions are playing
> a similar role in preparing our students for work life as did our early
> twentieth-century high schools in that less technically oriented era.
> (Federal Reserve Board, 2004)

Technological Developments and Workforce Globalization

Major technological developments, coupled with the globalization of the economy, had a broad effect on workforce education programs. The more specific origins of change were found in two areas. First was the continued application of microcomputer-based technologies, or information technology (IT), to many service, communications, and media operations. Second was the increased ability of overseas sources to provide products and services to U.S. markets. These trends started in the late 1990s and have continued to affect the present occupational structure and the skills needed to be successful (Friedman, 2006).

The IT expansion made it possible to end many forms of repetitive skilled and semiskilled work. Although the media tends to focus on the disappearance of jobs for steel workers and auto workers, there are equally important losses of clerical, book-keeping, and travel agent jobs. Many community college programs in manufacturing, communications, and clerical services were eliminated because they became irrelevant for job seekers (Levy & Murname, 2005).

Despite the effects of computer-based technologies and globalization, non-routine and semiskilled jobs still exist. Indeed, there is a continuing and sometimes growing demand for truck drivers, construction workers, automotive service technicians, and janitors. These jobs cannot be easily replaced by computers or sent overseas. Many of the allied health occupations also fit within these semiskilled but nonroutine categories. Although many community colleges offer programs in these occupations, they were not central to the trend toward investment in advanced technologies and the creation of advanced technology centers.

The second major development affecting workforce education in community colleges, in addition to computer-based technologies, is globalization of the workforce. Although this long-term trend began in the early 20th century, the speed and intensity of the process has increased considerably during the past decade. Original concerns about job loss focused on blue-collar occupations, but white-collar occupations, particularly those associated with IT, have also increasingly been affected. Call centers, programming operations, and engineering support centers proliferated through India, Pakistan, and other parts of Asia where English was widely spoken. Soon tax returns were being prepared and even medical and dental diagnoses were being rendered from overseas.

CURRENT TRENDS IN WORKFORCE EDUCATION PROGRAMS

Technical education, which has been central to the workforce mission of community colleges, is now in a period of transformation. A student preparing for a career in accounting can no longer depend on an associate degree to qualify for an entry-level position. The work previously done by entry-level employees has been automated, and the new work requires a university accounting degree. Clerical programs and mainframe computer language courses are becoming outmoded and are being replaced by industry certification programs such as those offered by Cisco and Microsoft. Design and drafting programs were subsumed by engineering programs as companies were outsourcing detailing work and leaving only design engineers within their companies. New occupational clusters are emerging in areas such as biotechnology, nanotechnology, alternative fuels, logistics, supply-chain management, and packaging. Skills in these areas are in demand, but this demand focuses more on the need for engineers, scientists, and people with postgraduate degrees. The demand for technicians and hands-on technical workers is still quite low in these new occupational clusters. It is apparent that major changes in curricula, instructor capabilities, and laboratory facilities will be necessary in order for community colleges to offer programs in these emerging occupational fields.

Even when community colleges have programs related to these high-technology occupations, they are significantly challenged to change, often to place more emphasis on science, mathematics, and communications. For example, companies might require a design engineer but no longer need a draftsperson because hands-on detailing is outsourced to a design center in a foreign country. As a result, community colleges might shift from drafting programs to pre-engineering programs.

Even traditional nursing programs are confronted with a growing differentiation of skill sets. Entry-level nurses can start with an associate degree, but career pathways into nursing specialization or research hospitals are trending toward requiring a 4-year or bachelor's degree. Many community college nursing programs have begun to develop ties with university nursing programs on the assumption that many students will continue their education beyond the associate level.

Another major step in the evolution of workforce education is the lessening of a commitment to programs that prepare people for entry-level work in many occupational fields. Especially hard hit are programs leading to entry-level manufacturing jobs and white-collar clerical positions. In some instances, colleges have cut off their investment in machining and welding equipment related to technical-level manufacturing programs. Advanced technology centers, which place more emphasis on the customized training of incumbent workers, have modified the approach to program investment through reliance on partnerships with corporations, business, and government.

In contrast, there has been a recent increase in enrollment in allied health programs, teacher education, and business IT. As the demand for health-care services continues to expand in most communities, hospitals and other health-care organizations continue to seek out partnerships with community colleges in many occupational areas. The traditional emphasis on nursing has been maintained, but with new emphasis on occupations such as certified nursing assistant, physical therapist, and medical records technician. Moreover, because health-care occupations are heavily regulated by state licensing requirements, there is a restricted labor supply (only those who pass the test can be employed), which gives community college programs a substantial role in health-care education.

The growth of teacher education programs is even more interesting. Salaries of public school teachers generally fail to compete with those of other professions despite the occupation's high education prerequisites. Although teaching as a career has become less attractive to middle- and upper-class students, community college students from lower-income backgrounds are attracted to its stability and relatively good salaries and benefits. During the past decade, teacher education programs in community colleges have flourished.

Meanwhile, community college certificate programs that provided students with technical skills but minimal general education and liberal arts courses have become less important as emerging occupations are more likely to require an associate degree and transfer to a university to obtain the needed qualifications. Many community colleges historically did not even assess the basic literacy skills of students seeking an occupational certificate. Today, it is important to place more emphasis on ensuring that all students develop the reading, writing, and math skills that will enable them to do college-level work and achieve at least an associate degree. For many occupations, career success will also require transfer to a 4-year college or university and a baccalaureate.

Another important trend is the growth of noncredit workforce development programs. Noncredit programs, whether they are called continuing education or adult education, have always been part of the community college. Traditionally, continuing education programs have offered a combination of language, job skills, entrepreneurship, cultural, arts and crafts, and personal interest programming. In the past decade, however, workforce development programs have grown to represent the bulk of the noncredit continuing education offerings. From 1995 to 2001, noncredit programs grew 8% faster than credit programs. A major stimulus for this growth was the development of IT certifications by technology vendors looking for proof of the skills necessary to perform in the new economy. These competency-based certification exams were viewed by the vendors and other employers as more dependable verification of acquired competencies than were other college certificates or degrees. They were rapidly adopted by community colleges, and within 5 years, about 25% of all community colleges were offering these vendor certification courses and exams. Although many colleges scaled back their activities after the dot-com boom went bust, many of the IT programs and classes remained in the noncredit areas and continued to grow in popularity and support (Jacobs & Grubb, 2006).

TWO DIVERGENT WORKFORCE EDUCATION TRENDS

There is a significant shift in credit programs away from entry-level work in traditional areas such as manufacturing toward occupational areas that require both a more substantial level of general education and ties to 4-year college degrees. The National Science Foundation's Advanced Technology Education initiative is an example of this shift. As a result, students in occupational areas are increasingly as likely as liberal arts students to transfer to a 4-year college or university and obtain a baccalaureate. This suggests the importance of the occupational certificate, and even the applied associate degrees might be diminished in the years ahead.

There is also, however, a substantial expansion of noncredit workforce education programming both in the areas of certification and customized job training for a specific business or group of businesses. These growing programs have been directed at incumbent workers who wish to improve their labor market credentials and advance on the job by acquiring specific skills. These programs tend to be taught by adjunct instructors or professional trainers hired by the college. The courses are therefore priced at market rates, which means that they can be considerably more expensive than usual tuition. These noncredit programs are little noticed by state policymakers or even by the leaders of the institutions that offer them, yet their size and impact can be considerable for the students and businesses that benefit from them as well as for the colleges that offer them. In states that financially support noncredit classes, enrollment in these programs can be as high as 15%–20% of the college's total (Van Noy & Jacobs, 2007).

Meeting these two divergent market demands—for increasingly advanced credit occupational programs and for noncredit competency-based instruction—means that colleges often maintain two relatively separate workforce development programs with two different staffs and two different missions. For the credit program, the mission is to provide a workforce to the local economy that matches the heightened skill requirements of employers. For the noncredit certification and customized job training programs, the mission is to enable participants to develop the specific competencies needed to undertake a specific work-related task or to prepare for career advancement. This evolving phenomenon—one college or two colleges—has implications for the way community colleges will organize and administer workforce education programs in the future.

SHIFTING STUDENT DEMOGRAPHICS IN WORKFORCE EDUCATION

In recent years, a change has been occurring in the demographics of students entering the traditional community college occupational programs. Essentially, more younger students are entering community colleges with the desire to transfer to 4-year colleges in the belief that the 4-year degree gives them the necessary mobility for a better job. They are avoiding occupational courses that they believe will not transfer, and because they seek the baccalaureate, they place less value on the associate degree. However, as young people exit these occupational programs, they are being replaced with adults beyond the traditional college-going age who seek increased job skills that they expect will lead to a well-paying job with career advancement potential. One interesting dimension of this demographic shift in workforce education enrollments is the effect of high school–to–community college transition programs. Programs such as Tech Prep and School to Work might make high school students more aware of the education requirements for various career pathways, leading them to select a university transfer program when they enroll at community colleges. The linkages between the vocational and technical programs at the secondary level and the career education programs at the community college level have never been strong, although recent national efforts such as the College and Career Transitions Initiative of the League for Innovation in the Community College demonstrate the potential benefits of strengthening the transition from high school to community college.

The first signs of this demographic shift from younger to older students were evident in the occupational flagship programs in nursing of the 1980s. At that time, few younger students applied to the programs, and nursing became a program in which older students enrolled to enter a career with good stability and steady income. The stereotype of the nursing student today is a woman, often a single head of household with young children, who needs a good-paying job to sustain her family. These women might not have done well in high school science and mathematics courses, and so they face the added challenge of taking basic biology and chemistry courses as well as developmental writing and math courses as they strive to meet the prerequisites for the nursing program. These women are often regarded as the heroes of the community college as they work together with their instructors to overcome great odds to achieve their career and family objectives.

The demographic shift in nursing was followed by similar shifts in IT, manufacturing, business, and marketing classes. These new students are older, often working full time and returning to school as a means of occupational mobility. Added to this demographic shift has been the growth of enrollment by immigrants from countries such as Mexico, Nigeria, India, and China who never went to U.S. high schools and who have considerable language challenges. The majority of these new Americans, especially those from Mexico, come from low-income backgrounds, so they face the additional challenge of finding sustainable work that permits them to support their families.

These older students understood the realities of the labor market and the need for education as one means of furthering their quest for sustainable wages. They chose community colleges because they were affordable, close to home, and offered class times compatible with work and family schedules. By the 1990s, many community college occupational courses, particularly in areas of manufacturing and business, were held only at night, indicating that the majority of the students were working adults.

CURRENT WORKFORCE EDUCATION CHALLENGES

The changing demographics of students have required a number of program and service changes to maintain and modernize the community college's open-door mission. Most obvious has been the number of students who need to improve their basic writing, math, reading, computer, and study skills. The traditional developmental or remedial classes often did not provide the literacy skills needed for college-level work. The conventional linear model of adult basic education programs leading to college developmental programs then college-level work was inappropriate for them. It raised the issues of whether learning could be accelerated and stages advanced through contextual learning (Brancard, Baker, & Jensen, 2006). Although these older students were highly motivated to learn new skills and often had substantial work-based learning experiences, colleges lacked any models to accelerate the learning of these students into the credit programs (Liebowitz & Taylor, 2004). In recent years, however, innovations in developmental education, such as intense summer programs, learning communities, and merged developmental education–occupational programs, have begun to address the unique needs of this student constituency.

An additional challenge was that this older student constituency not only lacked basic literacy skills but also often faced the difficult problem of balancing the roles of worker, family member, and student. Traditional student services, career counseling, and financial aid were not designed for their needs. Many had personal issues that often required more resources than colleges could muster. Some had criminal records that would make it difficult for them to find work. Others had issues with learning disabilities that were hard to isolate, let alone remediate. Other than the traditional short-term training for specific job skills offered through federal grants, there were few models that colleges could follow to take on the learning needs of these students.

A further challenge was faced by those for whom English was not their first language and those who took the noncredit route as the path to entry into the community college. Because they started their college work in noncredit classes such as ESL, they did not earn college credits that would lead to a degree and qualify them for student aid. The community college workforce education structure, which maintains separate credit and noncredit programs, was challenged by this constituency to develop new institutional pathways that start on the noncredit side and then make a reasonable transition to credit courses and programs. In some instances, colleges experimented with granting credit to some noncredit education if student progress was demonstrated. Indeed, in states such as California, with a large number of ESL students, more than 30% of the students in credit programs start on the noncredit side (California Community Colleges, 2007). It will be important to the future of workforce education that this transition from separate credit and noncredit paths be maintained and enhanced on a national basis.

PROMISING PRACTICES

The dilemma that the adult community college constituency poses to the future of workforce education programs is increasingly clear. How will colleges meet employers' demands for technical skills while also meeting the remedial needs of those for whom technical training is intended? The ability of community colleges to resolve these issues will ultimately determine the future of many for-credit workforce education programs. Although many colleges do not yet fully recognize that their response to these issues will determine the future of their workforce programs, let alone deal with them, there are some promising practices.

Breaking Through is a program of the National Council for Workforce Education and Jobs for the Future to promote and enhance the efforts of community colleges to help low-literacy adults prepare for and succeed in occupational and technical degree programs (Liebowitz & Taylor, 2004). Twenty-six community colleges are involved in this initiative, which is funded by the Charles Stewart Mott Foundation. It starts with the assumption that community colleges can play a role in helping low-income workers lift themselves out of poverty and achieve a higher standard of living. The participants strive to identify best practices of community colleges as they serve the workforce development needs of low-income working adults, most of whom seek basic education and literacy skills. Although many community colleges have extensive basic education and ESL programs, these are often disconnected from the rest of the college and staffed by people who are uninvolved in the college's central activities. As the demand for these courses increases, some colleges are taking a different approach, linking adult basic education not to GED or ESL programs but to the programs that motivate low-wage workers to attend community college in the first place: those that prepare students for increased success in the workplace.

Several community colleges have produced successful programs using this approach. Portland Community College has developed extensive consulting and wraparound services targeted for low-income adults. The Community College of Denver took a floundering city job training program for entry-level health-care workers, redesigned its curriculum, and produced college-ready workers in less than six months. Tacoma Community College integrated its ESL and early childhood education programs to help students earn credits toward a degree in child care. All of these innovations benefit low-wage workers by helping them increase their income and gain upward mobility in the job market.

The design elements in this strategy are well known. First, credit and non-credit programs are connected so that adults can move seamlessly into college (Perin & Charron, 2006). Many of these students cannot enter some of the occupational classes until they can improve their basic education skills. This is normally accomplished through the noncredit courses, but they must lead to credit classes. Second, the curriculum is contextual and relates directly to specific occupational fields. These are people who need jobs, and their initial interest in college is primarily because they believe it can get them better jobs. Third, support services do not stop at a specific literacy level but instead focus on clearly reaching the level needed to succeed in collegiate classes. Adult basic education becomes a feeder system for community college occupational programs. There are enormous advantages to this approach because it identifies a specific constituency that might be a market for many of the schools' entry-level workforce education programs. It also continues one of the important community college missions: serving people for whom a college education and a meaningful career would otherwise not be feasible to achieve.

※

Most community college students have career entry and advancement as the primary goal of their educational pursuits. For many, getting that first good, stable job with salary and benefits enough to support a family is an extremely important goal. Being a contributing member of the U.S. economy and earning a decent income is liberating because it opens the door to career advancement and opportunities for expression in other areas of life such as recreation, fitness, cultural activities, and lifelong learning. Yet the door of economic opportunity is at risk of closing for those with limited literacy and job skills.

The mismatch between the heightened workforce skill requirements of employers striving to compete in a global economy and the actual skills of employees and those seeking to enter the workforce is a general problem for the U.S. economy. This issue is especially pronounced as it relates to underprepared adults, many of whom are members of Hispanic, Black, and other minority groups that are the most educationally and economically disadvantaged. These underprepared adults look to the community college to empower them to find their way into the economic mainstream. Community colleges are positioning themselves as primary deliverers of workforce education in the face of a rapidly changing economy and the growth of enrollment by increasingly diverse students, many of whom are underprepared for career entry and advancement.

However, meeting the education needs of this constituency remains a challenge for community college presidents and other leaders. One of the major concerns is that added building-block programs such as noncredit adult education and developmental education programs will require large resources at the same time colleges are suffering significant cutbacks from state governments. Some colleges are, however, taking steps to see the large and growing number of low-income workers as an important constituency to be served as a part of their open-door commitment (see Liebowitz & Taylor, 2004). It is through programs such as Breaking Through that community colleges can reclaim their workforce education mission and give full expression to their open-door philosophy.

REFERENCES

Alssid, J. L., Gruber, D., Jenkins, D., Mazzeo, C., Roberts, B, & Stanback-Stroud, R. (2002, August). *Building a career pathways system: Promising practices in community college-centered workforce development.* New York: Workforce Strategy Center. Retrieved from http://www.workforcestrategy.org/publications/Career_Pathways.pdf

American Association of Community Colleges. (2006, August 4). *Mission statement.* Washington, DC: Author. Retrieved from http://www.aacc.nche.edu/About/Pages/mission.aspx

Belden Russonello & Stewart. (2004, September). *Expanding opportunity: Communicating about the role of community colleges.* Washington, DC: Author. Available from http://www.brspoll.com/reports.htm

Brancard, R., Baker, E. D., & Jensen, L. (2006). *Accelerated developmental education* project: Research report: Community College of Denver. Retrieved from http://www.communitycollegecentral.org/Resources/research/Materials/CCDLuminaAcceleratedResearchReport62106.pdf

California Community Colleges System Office. (2007). *Focus on results: Accountability reporting for the California community colleges: A report to the legislature, pursuant to AB 1417.* Sacramento, CA: Author. Retrieved from http://www.cccco.edu/Portals/4/TRIS/research/ARCC/arcc_report_2007.pdf

Carnevale, A. P., & Rose, S. J. (1998) *Education for what? The new office economy.* Princeton, NJ: Educational Testing Service. (ERIC # ED452344)

Cohen, A. M., & Brawer, F. B. (1996). *The American community college* (3rd ed.). San Francisco: Jossey Bass. (ERIC # ED389384)

Dougherty, K. J. (1994). *The contradictory college: The conflicting origins, impacts, and futures of the community college.* Albany, NY: State University of New York Press.

Federal Reserve Board. (2004, March 11). *Testimony of Chairman Alan Greenspan. Education.* Before the Committee on Education and the Workforce, U.S. House of Representatives. Retrieved from http://www.federalreserve.gov/boarddocs/testimony/2004/20040311/default.htm

Friedman, T. L. (2006). *The world is flat: A brief history of the twenty-first century* (2nd ed.). New York: Farrar, Straus, and Giroux.

Jacobs, J. (1989). Training the workforce of the future. *Technology Review, 92*(6).

Jacobs, J. (2001, Fall). Community colleges and the Workforce Investment Act: Promises and problems of the new vocationalism. *New Directions for Community Colleges, 2001*(115), 93–100. (ERIC # EJ654310)

Jacobs, J., & Fasenfest, D. (2000, June 15–17). Revival and change in the automobile industry of southeast Michigan. In I. Johansson & R. Dahlberg (Eds.), *Entrepreneurship, firm growth, and regional development in the new economic geography: Papers presented at Uddevalla Symposium 2000, 15-17 June 2000, Trollhattan, Sweden* (pp. 257–282). Uddevalla, Sweden: University of Trolhättan.

Jacobs, J., & Grubb, W. N. (2006). The limits of "training for now": Lessons from information technology certification. In T. Bailey & V. Smith Morest (Eds.), *Defending the community college equity agenda* (pp. 132–154). Baltimore: Johns Hopkins University Press.

Karp, M. M., Jacobs, J., & Hughes, K. (2003). *Credentials, curriculum, and access: The debate over nurse preparation.* Washington, DC: Community College Press. (ERIC # ED471128)

Levy, F., & Murname, R. J. (2004). *The new division of labor: How computers are creating the next job market.* Princeton, NJ: Princeton University Press.

Liebowitz, M., & Taylor, J. C. (2004, November). *Breaking through: Helping low-skilled adults enter and succeed in college and careers.* Boston: Jobs For the Future and National Council for Workforce Education. Retrieved from http://

www.ncwe.org/documents/report_2004_ncweJff_breakingThrough.pdf

Office of Technology Assessment. (1990). *Worker training: Competing in the new international economy* (OTA-ITE-457). Washington, DC: U.S. Government Printing Office.

Perin, D., & Charron, K. (2006). Lights just click on every day. In T. Bailey & V. Smith Morest (Eds.), *Defending the community college equity agenda* (pp. 155–194). Baltimore: Johns Hopkins University Press.

Prince, D., & Jenkins, D. (2005). *Building pathways to success for low skilled adult students: Lessons for community college policy and practice from a statewide longitudinal study.* New York: Community College Research Center. (ERIC # ED485342)

Van Noy, M., & Jacobs, J. (2007). *Clarifying the landscape of noncredit workforce education.* Unpublished manuscript.

Chapter 11

Reinventing Career Pathways and Continuing Education

Laurance J. Warford

The community college is an American success story. No academic institution has done more in recent decades to democratize higher education. Community colleges have been the leading providers of career and continuing education for the masses in this country, including minorities and other previously disenfranchised groups. A major part of this success comes from their comprehensive, lifelong workforce education and continuing education offerings. Millions of people are served at different stages of their lives and at varied junctures in their career progression. Yet despite its history as the nation's premier open-door higher education institution, there is so much more for the community college to do to be a primary player in providing the highly skilled workforce needed for the United States to compete in a global marketplace. The challenge for community colleges is to empower the very groups that education has historically not served well to achieve their career and academic goals and therefore increase the competitiveness of the U.S. economy. The nation's economic and social future depends on empowering Hispanics, Blacks, recent immigrants, and others who experience barriers to career success to develop the skills they need to enter and progress in the workforce.

Reinvention of the workforce and continuing education functions of the community college takes on an entirely new meaning when one considers these factors:

- Nearly everyone who seeks postsecondary education does so to prepare for their life's work.

- Most people will have five to seven careers in their lifetimes.
- Education and work are not linear; people move into and out of education all of their lives.
- Each time there is a career change or even a job change, it is likely that additional education is required.
- The community college has been dubbed *the new graduate school* because many people with degrees return there for additional education to prepare for career advancement or to shift careers.

REASSESSING GOALS TO MEET NEW WORKFORCE DEMANDS

In a report from the Greater Expectations National Panel, formed by the Association of American Colleges and Universities, the authors suggested that community colleges need to erase "the artificial distinctions between studies deemed liberal (interpreted to mean that they are not related to job training) and those called practical (which are assumed to be)" (AACU, 2002, p. 26). The panel report continued, "A liberal education *is* a practical education because it develops just those capacities needed by every thinking adult: analytical skills, effective communications, practical intelligence, ethical judgment, and social responsibility" (AACU, 2002, p. 26).

A liberal education, which develops common capabilities needed for all careers, can blend powerfully with career education programs that meet the heightened job-specific skill requirements of our technology-oriented economy. Those involved in advanced workforce training are increasingly sensing the demands of employers for rigorous career and academic courses to ensure that people leave each segment of education prepared to be successful in work and life. In 2005, during a meeting of the Community College Workforce Partnership Network Advisory Working Group, a group of community college presidents and officials of the League for Innovation in the Community College found that employers expect community colleges not only to train students to survive in the workplace, but to thrive as well.

Accordingly, one can see the similarities among workforce training in a community college, a medical internship in a research university, and a teacher education program at a regional 4-year college. Are all these students preparing for their life's work, and will they be part of the workforce? Have we placed artificial distinctions between academic or liberal education and vocational or career technical education? Does this serve the learner well? Does it serve this country well?

Terry O'Banion, former president and CEO of the League for Innovation in the Community College, provided leadership in encouraging community colleges to become more learning centered. He suggested that such efforts "reflect the reforms taking place in traditional higher education" and that "American education must continue to overhaul its outdated, traditional framework restricted by time, place, bureaucracy and limited teacher roles" (O'Banion, 1997). O'Banion's work and that of other community college leaders suggests that we must focus on achieving the learning outcomes sought by learners and by those who employ them. We must become learning colleges where students achieve their career objectives and the college continuously improves its programs, services, and systems. That being the case, how do we reinvent community college career–technical and continuing education to meet this lofty objective? There is ample evidence that we must reform our systems of education and workforce training in this country. As a prelude, however, it is important to understand the international and national economic and workforce environment within which community colleges operate.

Thomas Friedman's book, *The World is Flat,* is one of the most frequently cited publications on the need to understand what is going on in the world economy. Friedman (2006) indicates that developing countries like India and China are exploiting technological advances to provide workforce access for growing numbers of their large populations. Whereas the United States has a workforce shortage and mismatch between the skill requirements of employers and actual skills of workers, other nations have workforce surpluses and are becoming quite competitive in the world marketplace. In *The Flight of the Creative Class,* Florida (2005) pointed out that there is international competition for workforce talent, and the United States no longer attracts the immigrant talent that it once did.

According to a report of a new Commission on the Skills of the American Workforce, *Tough Choices or Tough Times* (National Center on Education and the Economy [NCEE], 2007), when an earlier commission released its 1990 findings (NCEE, 1990), the globalization of the world's economy was just getting underway. The 1990 report indicated that a worldwide market was developing for low-skill labor and that work would go to countries with the lowest labor costs. It indicated that the best choice for our country in the early 1990s was to abandon the low-skill market and compete worldwide for high-value-added products and services. The commission pointed out that to do so, the United States would have to adopt international standards for educating its workers "because only countries with high-skilled workforces could successfully compete in that market" (NCEE, 2007).

What has happened since 1990? The United States is now competing with countries that can "offer large numbers of highly educated employees who are willing to work for low wages" and that "China and India are only the tip of the iceberg" (NCEE, 2007, p. xvi). Whereas the United States could once take pride in having the largest and best-educated workforce, it is now being surpassed in the proportion of its entering workforce that has the equivalent of a high school diploma. The commission concluded: "The core problem is that our education and training systems were built for another era…. We can get where we must go only by changing the system itself" (NCEE, 2007, p. xix).

CONNECTEDNESS, COLLABORATION, AND TRANSITION: REFORMING THE SYSTEM

The U.S. education system is actually a series of systems and silos: K–12, community colleges, and higher education are often administered, funded, and governed by separate agencies. Funding systems are often targeted at certain populations or provide subsidies for certain endeavors. The divisions between academic and vocational education are perpetuated in part by federal and state funding streams. In community colleges, divisions exist between academic and vocational education and between credit and noncredit offerings. Continuing education is often a division considered by many to be peripheral to the main missions of the community college. In addition, educators and employers do not work effectively together as a general rule. Although those of us in education indicate that we seek the advice and participation of employers, studies show that we often lack the ability to bring the education and work worlds together in an effective manner.

This pervasive lack of connectedness and collaboration, intentional or not, is having a devastating negative effect on the success of students. Only 67 of 100 students who begin ninth grade in this country will graduate from high school (Ewell, Jones, & Kelly, 2003). In an era when most agree that some postsecondary education is required for a good job and career advancement, one third of our youth are failing to take even the first critical step toward earning a good living by completing high school. An equally troubling trend has been reported by Richard Kazis, senior vice-president of Jobs for the Future. He reported that progress in expanding education attainment has hit a plateau in this country. The high school graduation rate peaked in 1970 at 77% and has since remained stagnant, primarily because of rapid growth in groups of students that the education system serves less well, such as immigrants, Hispanics, Blacks, those with physical limitations, and those from low-income families. Today, 50% of low-income students enroll in a college program, compared to 89% of upper-income students (Kazis, 2003).

The statistics do not get better in terms of how young people fare in college work—especially in community colleges. In conducting its study, "The Bridge Project: Strengthening K–16 Transition Policies," the Stanford University Research Center presented some distressing statistics, including the fact that 63% of recent high school graduates entering community college have to take at least one remedial course in math, reading, or writing. In urban community colleges, this rate of remediation can be as great as 75% (Venezia, Kirst, & Antinio, 2004). These distressing statistics belie the fact that most students have high aspirations for their lives.

The Stanford study indicated that 80% of eighth graders expect to go to postsecondary education, but only 70% of high school graduates go to college within two years of graduation. According to the study, those aspirations are being undermined by disconnected education systems and other barriers. Students who need the most support to advance their careers and academic goals are not getting it. Some of the cross-institutional shortcomings that create barriers to student success are the following:

- Students, parents, and K–12 educators get conflicting and vague messages about what students need to know to enter and succeed in college.
- Course work between high school and college is often not connected.
- Students graduate from high school under one set of standards and three months later are required to meet a whole new set of standards in college.
- Current data systems are not equipped to address students' needs across systems.
- No one is held accountable for issues related to student transitions from high school to college (Venezia et al., 2004).

The Stanford Bridge Project study concluded that "while educators and policymakers share the common goal of improving student performance, they often act in isolation; thus, efforts are sometimes conflicting or duplicated, and often certain needs are never addressed" (Stanford University, 2006).

In the past, community colleges have been criticized for "cooling out" the academic aspirations of students who were underprepared for college-level studies. These students gradually came to feel that college was not appropriate for them, even if they had the potential (Clark, 1960). According to sociologist James Rosenbaum, much of this criticism is misplaced. Students' failures arise not so much from barriers inside colleges but from an inter-institutional failure caused by the lack of connectedness between high school and college. Community colleges and the public schools have failed to convey clear information about the preparation that high school students need for success in college (Rosenbaum, 1999). Reinvention of workforce strategies in the community college must address the apparent lack of connectedness, collaboration, and effectiveness in transitioning students successfully from secondary to postsecondary education and on to careers. This is critical because nearly half of all students who enter 2-year institutions do not return for their second year, and the gap of college entry between high- and low-income students has not narrowed in three decades (Kazis, 2003).

Kazis (2003) reported that, in view of demographic trends, the situation is likely to grow worse unless changes are made in state policy and local practice. The fastest-growing segments of the high school and college-age populations have the greatest academic disadvantages. When viewed from the perspective of an impending serious workforce shortage in this country, these statistics take on a greater significance. The U.S. population is aging—by 2050, people older than 55 will constitute 38% of the population, compared with 27% in 2000. Minority groups are growing faster than the White majority. By 2050, Whites will constitute less than 50% of the U.S. population. Thus, between now and then, there will be a disproportionate increase of minorities in the younger groups (Carlson, 2004). In other words, as the U.S. population ages, the younger groups both decline in relative size and become increasingly composed of minorities. Thus, the very people we are depending on to be our workforce in global competition are the most challenged, and they are finding limited success in our education system.

FACTORING IN AN AGING WORKFORCE

Any discussion of reinventing the workforce must take into account that a majority of the people who will be working in 2020 are already doing so. Community colleges must consider improved solutions if they are to serve the adult workforce and improve how they fare in the U.S. education system. Here are some facts to consider as the United States falls behind other countries in education attainment and workforce readiness:

- About half of the adult workforce (80–90 million) do not have the basic education and communication skills required to get or advance in a job that will pay a family-sustaining wage (Council for Advancement of Adult Literacy [CAAL], 2008).
- This nation's workforce includes 54 million adults who lack a college degree, and of those, 34 million have no college experience at all (CAAL, 2008).
- A high percentage of students who enroll in adult basic education or study to obtain a GED certificate never enroll in a college credit program (Jenkins, Zeidenberg, & Kienzl, 2009).

If the current trends hold, the United States will continue to trail global competitors on a number of key measures of education achievement. Pusser et al. (2007) stated that "With a committed and informed approach, we can help realize the vast educational potential of America's adult learners.... If we ignore the problem, we will further limit our adult citizens and erode the vitality of our essential institutions." It is clear that academic preparation, workforce education, and continuing education should be considered in context with one other. Lifelong learning is no longer an option, as people will be in and out of education throughout their lives.

A CAREER PATHWAYS MODEL FOR COMMUNITY COLLEGES

Leadership is being provided at the national level on many fronts regarding reform of our education and training systems. Scott Hess of the U.S. Department of Education, Office of Vocational and Adult Education (OVAE), recently wrote, "Recognizing the dilemma facing today's students and eventual employers, virtually every organization overseeing secondary and postsecondary education at the national, state, and local levels has initiated policies and programs to find solutions to changing education and workforce challenges" (cited in Warford, 2006, p. 15). Hess pointed out that although mission and vision statements in strategic plans have always been focused on preparing all students for their future careers, there is a misalignment between mission statements and actual program delivery. He said, "What seems either vague or absent in many plans…is the way all students are to be provided these opportunities, and the extent to which all student career goals and interests will be aligned with program options" (cited in Warford, 2006, p. 15).

Table 11.1 Career Clusters and Pathways Developed by the Office of Vocational and Adult Education	
Career Clusters and Pathways	
1. Agriculture, Food, and Natural Resources • power, structural, and technical systems • national resource systems • agribusiness systems • environmental service systems • plant systems • animal systems • food products and processing systems	**5. Hospitality and Tourism** • restaurants and food and beverage service • recreation, amusements, and attractions • travel and tourism • lodging
2. Architecture and Construction • design/pre-construction • construction • maintenance/operations	**6. Human Services** • counseling and mental health services • family and community services • personal care services • consumer services • early childhood development
3. Arts/Audiovisual Technology and Communications • visual arts • performing arts • journalism and broadcasting • audio and video technology and film • printing technologies • telecommunication technologies	**7. Information Technology** • network systems • programming and software development • interactive media • information support and services
	8. Science, Technology, Engineering, and Mathematics • science and math • engineering and technology
4. Business Management and Administration • human resources • management • business financial management and accounting • marketing • administration and information support • business analysis	**9. Education and Training** • teaching and training • professional support services • administration and administrative support

Career Clusters and Pathways

10. Finance
- business financial management
- banking and related services
- financial and investment planning
- insurance services

11. Government and Public Administration
- governance
- national security
- foreign service
- planning
- revenue and taxation
- regulation
- public management and administration

12. Health Science
- therapeutic services
- diagnostic services
- health informatics
- support services
- biotechnology research and development

13. Law, Public Safety, and Security
- legal services
- emergency and fire management services
- correction services
- law enforcement services
- security and protective services

14. Manufacturing
- production
- manufacturing production process development
- maintenance, installation, and repair
- quality assurance
- logistics and inventory control
- health safety and environmental assurance

15. Marketing, Sales, and Service
- marketing information management and research
- marketing communications and promotion
- professional sales and marketing
- management and entrepreneurship
- buying and merchandising
- e-marketing
- distribution and logistics

16. Transportation, Distribution, and Logistics
- warehousing and distribution center operations
- logistics planning and management services
- facility and mobile equipment maintenance
- transportation operations
- transportation systems/infrastructure planning, management and regulation
- health safety and environmental management
- sales and services

Note. Adapted from Warford (2006) with permission.

OVAE has provided leadership and funding for two major initiatives emphasizing strong partnerships linking secondary and postsecondary education with employers and other significant organizations. Two critical components have been addressed: (1) the need for a common organizational structure that defines career technical education as an important part of all education plans and (2) the need for a common definition for career pathways, including models that outline rigorous academic and career course sequences in high school and college. Through the leadership of various states and secondary schools in partnership with colleges, employers, and other important organizations, 16 career clusters have been developed, with two main sets of standards. The first set identifies the knowledge and skills needed for all occupations within the entire cluster. These standards are organized into 10 categories established in agreement by all 16 cluster groups. All students who master the foundation standards will do so in the context of their chosen cluster area. If students change their career focus—and many will—to another cluster area, they will still have been exposed to the 10 categories of knowledge and skills.

The second set of standards identifies subsets within the 16 career clusters. These subsets more narrowly group the occupations within the clusters into pathways. As in the broader cluster standards, the pathway standards identify the knowledge and skills needed for each of the occupations within. There are 81 identified career pathways, as illustrated in Table 11.1. The importance of the pathway standards is that, whether they are used for a specific pathway or combined with other pathways to develop curricula, they will be based on standards validated by employers. Thus postsecondary and secondary educators can work together to link course work in both education levels that will lead to successful careers.

A second major initiative of OVAE is the College and Career Transitions Initiative (CCTI), which is administered by the League for Innovation in the Community College. CCTI is a community college–led initiative that focuses on collaboration with secondary and higher education and employers to develop model career pathways. CCTI has produced model templates in five of the 16 clusters as well as sample templates for all 81 career pathways. The templates have become the model for many state-level initiatives to reform career technical education. CCTI has five primary anticipated outcomes (League, 2009):

- Decreased need for remediation at the postsecondary level.
- Increased enrollment and persistence in postsecondary education.
- Increased academic and skill achievement at the secondary and postsecondary levels.
- Increased attainment of postsecondary degrees, certificates, or other recognized credentials.
- Increased entry into employment or further education.

Fifteen community college–led site partnerships (which included secondary schools and employers and often 4-year colleges and universities and other important organizations) were selected to develop the CCTI career pathways using the model templates. Their work was organized around an improvement plan with the five major outcomes as goals. This work has led to the formation of the CCTI Network, which is open to all community colleges that have an interest in developing career pathways for student success. Members of the network represent more than 40 states and several foreign countries (see the League's Web site at http://www. league.org).

A model to guide community colleges as they reinvent the career pathways aspects of the open door takes on greater meaning when applied to diverse students. An effective career pathways model must serve not only recent high school graduates but also other constituencies such as high school students, out-of-school youth, workers, unemployed or underemployed people, and former inmates. To address these challenges, a panel of 25 leading educators worked with the League for Innovation in the Community College to develop a systemic framework of career pathways. This panel concluded that we must reinvent education for student success in colleges and careers, defining a career pathway as follows:

> A career pathway is a framework for connecting a series of educational programs with integrated work experience and support services, thereby enabling students and workers to combine school and work and advance over time to better jobs and higher levels of education and training. Career and technical education (CTE) in secondary education serves as the launch pad for students in their transition to postsecondary education and enhanced training opportunities. (League, 2007, p. 3)

This career pathways model is designed to accomplish the following:

- Target regional labor markets, focus on employment sectors, and provide a framework for workforce development by integrating the programs and resources of community colleges and other education institutions, workforce agencies, and social service providers.
- Align with the needs and informed interests of students and workers.
- Provide community colleges the opportunity to link academic course work to the local economy while meeting the varied needs and informed interests of the diverse students they serve. (League, 2007, p. 3)

Career pathways thus provide a systemic framework for the reinvention of the way community colleges approach workforce education, continuing education, and training. They provide a new way of doing business with secondary schools and employers. The goal stated by the League is as follows:

> The ultimate goal is for career pathways to provide a seamless system of career exploration, preparation, and skill upgrades linked to academic credits and credentials, available with multiple entry and exit points spanning middle school, secondary school, postsecondary

institutions, adult education and workplace education. (League, 2007, p. 3)

Career pathways can be combined as an integral part of many initiatives to reform and reinvent workforce training at all levels. They provide a systemic framework for transforming educational institutions in a way that actively meets the changing needs of employers and the informed education needs and interests of students and workers across the learning continuum. From a program perspective, several factors have contributed to this evolving understanding of the potential of career pathways to lead reinvention and change:

- "A growing awareness of the need for demand-driven and sustained partnerships among community colleges, business, workforce, and economic development, and community leaders focused on meeting regional, sector-based workforce needs.
- A shift from seeking best-practice models to an approach that evaluates all activities from planning to continuous improvement based on measurable outcomes and established feedback mechanisms.
- Evolving models of sustainability as state and federal policies align and encourage connections between students, careers, the labor market, and economic development, allowing multiple funding sources to be blended to cultivate continuity.
- The need for secondary schools to eliminate a two-track system, to a system that provides opportunities for all students to make a transition successfully to postsecondary education in both academic and career-related studies.
- The emergence of career pathways as a critical economic development tool. With globalization of the workforce, intellectual talent can be located almost anywhere on earth. Extensive research and literature suggest the communities, regions, and states that will be most competitive are those that support and grow industry clusters based on demand. One critical component of this strategy is the growth of human capital. Since career pathways are focused around regional or statewide industry sectors and not a single business, the development of career pathways presents a strategic advantage in supplying the talent needed by business and industry, from entry-level technicians to scientists and engineers." (League, 2007, p. 5)

The core elements of the comprehensive career pathways framework outlined by the League can be an excellent tool as community colleges reinvent their career and continuing education programs to better serve the diverse students knocking at their doors. The features and components of each of the six core elements are listed in Table 11.2.

Table 11.2 Features and Components of the Comprehensive Career Pathways Framework

Features	Components
Core Element 1: Institutional and Instructional Transformation	
Mission integration	Collaborative design: Breaking down the silos of academic, student support, remedial, continuing education and workforce development to create a unified system.
	Strong, focused partnerships: Secondary school partnerships that focus on seamless high school to college transitions.
Curriculum and instructional transformation	Alternative delivery systems: Flexibility in time, place and method of instruction, including distance learning, workplace learning and blended delivery modes.
	Contexted curriculum: Infusing industry-based and career-relevant material into developmental education, GED, basic adult education and ESL programs.
	Modularized, or chunked, curriculum: Curriculum segmented into modules with multiple entry and exit points.
	Competency-based curriculum: Curriculum design based on industry skill standards and job-related competencies.
	Common organizational structure for career technical education at the secondary level: The 16 career clusters as the organizing tool for secondary career technical programs.
Visual roadmaps and templates	Navigation tools: Roadmaps or templates to provide students and workers with visual information on the courses and competencies needed for specific occupations.
	Career lattices or patterns: Illustrations to enable students and workers to visualize the patterns of lateral and vertical movement within an occupation or career cluster.
	Inclusive development processes: Engagement of employers, faculty members, industry advisors, educational administrators and labor representatives in designing skills-driven curriculum.
	Tool accessibility: Navigation visuals and other tools made widely available to students, advisors, counselors, parents, workers and workforce professionals through Web sites, career guides, college catalogs, etc.
Articulation and transition	Bridge programs: Inclusion in developmental education programs of career-related content that provides a bridge between learning basic literacy skills and moving to credit-bearing career education courses.
	Rigorous academic credentials: Programs that produce occupational credentials that are rigorous, recognizable and relevant to the labor market.
	Dual or concurrent enrollment and dual credit: Provision of opportunities for secondary students to earn college credits through dual enrollment at a community college
	Articulation agreements: Provision of seamless articulation across educational institutions for courses, credentials, certificates and degrees.
Core Element 2: Student Supports and Tools	
Career planning and counseling	Career planning resources: Provision of career planning courses and workshops including tools such as assessment, career portfolios and individual career planning.

Table 11.2 Features and Components of the Comprehensive Career Pathways Framework (Cont'd)

Features	Components
Core Element 2: Student Supports and Tools (cont'd)	
Career planning and counseling	Job-seeking resources: Provision of job search assistance to enhance skills such as resume writing, interviewing and social networking.
Internships	Inclusion in career education programs of the opportunity for internships, co-op work experience and other methods of learning by doing
College and workforce readiness preparation	Provision to secondary students of supportive services that enhance college and workforce readiness such as placement-test preparation workshops and summer literacy skill development programs.
Case management	Provision of individual support to students with transportation, child care and financial concerns, including referral to community agencies
Credit for prior and experiential learning	Provision of clearly defined options for adults to continue lifelong learning and receive credit for prior experience.
Core Element 3: Partnerships That Drive Planning and Implementation	
Inclusive involvement	Involvement of employers, business organizations, labor organizations, educational institutions, economic development organizations, etc. in meaningful partnerships that connect all partners in a unified workforce development system.
Collaboration and trust	Nurturing of trust among partners through shared leadership, planning, program development and implementation, and continuous improvement.
Demand-driven economic development strategy	Designing demand-driven career education programs that support local economic development by linking the skills developed by students directly to the job skill requirements of employers.
Core Element 4: Employer Involvement	
Employer validation of career pathways	Involvement of employers in validating that a career pathway is relevant to the local labor market.
Employer involvement in the determination of relevant skills and competencies	Involvement of employers in ensuring that the skills and competencies of career education programs match the job skill requirements of local businesses, and in determining whether the planned skills and competencies build on one another to enable entry and movement in a career pathway.
Ongoing oversight of pathway relevance and content	Involvement of employers in the continuous assessment and updating of career pathways programs.
Employer input and support for incumbent worker pathways	Involvement of employers in customizing career pathways programs to meet the specialized needs of adults already in the workforce.
Employer support of pathways graduates	Involvement of employers in supporting and using the local pipeline of career pathways graduates as they seek meaningful jobs and careers.

Features	Components
Table 11.2 Features and Components of the Comprehensive Career Pathways Framework (Cont'd)	
Core Element 5: Continuous Improvement	
Planning	Involvement of community partners in assessing current and future workforce demands as the basis for career pathway design
Accountability	Use of the measurement of actual student learning outcomes as compared to employer skill requirements as the basis for being held accountable by employers and for involving employers in continuous improvement.
Core Element 6: Sustainability	
Leadership at all levels and cross-sections	Engagement of bottom-up as well as top-down leadership (from governing boards to workers on the factory floor) in the partner organizations.
Replicable models	Development of career pathway models that are replicable in other institutions and regions as a means of leveraging resources and sustainability
Reallocating and blending multiple funding sources	Reallocation: Reallocation of college and school district resources to support career pathways development;
	Blending: Blending private and regional, state and federal funds to foster shared commitment and leverage resources.
Alignment of state and federal policy	Alignment of state and federal career pathways policies (high school graduation requirements, college readiness, dual enrollment, etc.) to support unified local and regional career pathways initiatives of secondary schools, community colleges, other colleges and universities, employers and other community organizations.
Note. Adapted from League (2007) with permission.	

The stakes are high. Community colleges must reinvent and realign their workforce and continuing education systems for a new era. If the open door of educational opportunity is to have real meaning in this new era, colleges must be fully engaged with the increasingly diverse student constituencies of the current and future workforce. The fastest-growing student constituencies such as minorities, women, older learners, first-generation learners, and immigrants are in general the most challenged in terms of educational and career success. Colleges must seek new alternatives and ways of viewing the preparation of people for the careers that they will have throughout their lifetimes. The majority of these diverse students do not aspire to become university professors or spend their lifetimes in academia; they attend college to get a good job and prepare for career advancement. As research indicates, just going to college loses value when preparation for a practical outcome—a career—does not happen.

Kay McClenney, the director of the Community College Survey of Student Engagement, talked about the importance of reinvention and foundational change in her keynote address to those attending the CCTI Summit:

A reasonable person might well ask this question: Why is this work—the work of developing career pathways, of creating seamless transitions for students from high school to community colleges and further education—so important? Why does it really matter?

The succinct and straightforward answer is this: The whole future of our communities and of our country, not to mention countless individuals, depends significantly on the ability of community and technical colleges—along with their partners in education and the employer community—to do a far better job of moving students to and through our institutions, toward better jobs, toward continuing education over a lifetime. (McClenney, 2006)

REFERENCES

Association of American Colleges and Universities. (2002). *Greater expectations: A new vision for learning as a nation goes to college.* Washington, DC: Author. (ERIC # ED468787)

Carlson, B. (2004). *Why CCTI is so important.* Keynote address presented at the meeting of the College and Career Transitions Initiative, Largo, MD.

Clark, B. (1960). The "cooling-out" function in higher education. *American Journal of Sociology.* 65(6), 569–576. Retrieved from http://faculty.washington.edu/rsoder/EDUC310/571BurtonClarkCoolingOut.pdf

Council for Advancement of Adult Literacy for the National Commission on Adult Literacy. (2008). *Reach higher, America: Overcoming crisis in the U.S. workforce.* Washington, DC: Author.

Ewell, P. T., Jones, D. P., & Kelly, P. J. (2003). *Conceptualizing and researching the educational pipeline.* Boulder, CO: National Center for Higher Education Management Systems. Retrieved from http://www.higheredinfo.org/analyses/Pipeline%20Article.pdf

Florida, R. (2005). *The flight of the creative class: The new global competition for talent.* New York: HarperCollins.

Friedman, T. L. (2006). *The world is flat: A brief history of the twenty-first century* (2nd ed.). New York: Farrar, Straus, and Giroux.

Jenkins, D., Zeidenberg, M., & Kienzl, G. S. (2009). *Educational outcomes of I-BEST, Washington State Community and Technical College System's integrated education and skills training program; Findings from a multivariate analysis.* New York, NY: Columbia University Teachers College, Community College

Research Center.

Kazis, R. (2003). *Ready for tomorrow: Helping all students achieve secondary and post-secondary success: A guide for governors.* Washington, DC: National Governors Association. Retrieved from http://www.nga.org/cda/files/0310READY.pdf

League for Innovation in the Community College. (2007). *Career pathways as a systemic framework: Rethinking education for student success in college and careers.* Phoenix, AZ: Author. Retrieved from http://www.league.org/league/projects/ccti/files/Systemic_Framework.pdf

League for Innovation in the Community College. (2009). *Anticipated outcomes of the CCTI.* Retrieved from http://www.league.org/league/projects/ccti/objectives.html

McClenney, K. (2006, March). *Pathways to student success.* Keynote address presented at the CCTI Summit, Phoenix, AZ. Retrieved from http://www.league.org/league/projects/CCTI/summit/2006/mcclenney.doc

National Center on Education and the Economy. (1990). *America's choice: High skills or low wages! The report of the commission on the skills of the American workforce.* Rochester, NY: Author.

National Center on Education and the Economy. (2007). *Tough choices or tough times: The report of the new commission on the skills of the American workforce.* San Francisco: Jossey-Bass.

O'Banion, Terry (1997). *Creating more learning centered community colleges.* Newport Beach, CA: League for Innovation in the Community College. (ERIC # ED414980)

Pusser, B., Breneman, D. W., Gansneder, B. M., Kohl, K. J., Levin, J. S., Milam, J. H., & Turner, S. E. (2007, March). *Returning to learning: Adults' success in college is key to America's future.* Indianapolis, IN: Lumina Foundation for Education. Available from the Lumina Foundation Web site: http://www.luminafoundation.org

Rosenbaum, J. E. (1999). *Unrealistic plans and misdirected efforts: Are community colleges getting the right message to high school students?* New York: Community College Research Center. (ERIC # ED428975)

Stanford University Research Center. (2006). *The bridge project.* Retrieved from http://www.stanford.edu/group/bridgeproject/

Venezia, A., Kirst, M. W., & Antinio, A. L. (2003). *Betraying the college dream: How disconnected K–12 and postsecondary education systems undermine student aspirations.* Stanford, CA: Stanford Institute for Higher Education Research. Retrieved from http://www.stanford.edu/group/bridgeproject/betrayingthecollegedream.pdf

Warford, L. J. (Ed.). (2006). *Pathways to student success: Case studies from the College and Career Transitions Initiative.* Phoenix, AZ: League for Innovation in the Community College. Retrieved from http://www.league.org/league/projects/ccti/files/CCTI_Pathway_Book.pdf

Chapter 12

Reinventing the Open Door Through National Leadership

Shawna J. Forbes and Brian Singleton

National organizations dedicated to promoting the democratic ideal of universal higher education access and success have been a major driving force for community colleges. State and national associations, foundations, universities, government units, nonprofit agencies, community college organizations, and business groups have led by taking balcony-view or big-picture initiatives to complement the grassroots efforts of individual community colleges. These state and national organizations have influenced changes in state and national public policy, enhanced community college leadership and professional development, led research and evaluation projects, strengthened financial aid programs, and provided grants to individual colleges and college consortia to develop best practices that could be emulated by other community colleges. They have also enlisted the schools in state and national efforts to address economic, education, social, and cultural challenges such as global economic competitiveness, skills gaps in the workforce, the growing academic achievement gap between some minorities and the general population, the alienation of urban Black men, and the resegregation of urban public schools.

During the past decade, a considerable array of state and national programs has emerged that support and nurture community colleges in their efforts to effectively serve diverse students. These organizations have advocated fundamental change in areas such as developmental education, high school–to–community college transition, career education and workforce development, tutorial programs and other forms of supplemental education, student services, and community college–to–university transfer initiatives. Taken as a whole, these national initiatives have as their primary focus innovation and transformation that embraces all four elements of the open-door model: student access, student success, inclusiveness, and community engagement.

EXAMPLES OF OPEN-DOOR INITIATIVES SPONSORED BY NATIONAL ORGANIZATIONS

The American Association of Community Colleges

AACC is a central, national force for advancing the open-door philosophy and practice of the community college, and it is arguably the glue that holds all national efforts together. AACC's mission speaks directly to student access and success: "Building a nation of learners by advancing America's community colleges" (AACC, 2006). More specifically, three of the AACC's five strategic action areas directly address open-door objectives: student access, learning, and success; economic and workforce development; and global and intercultural education. The other two strategic action areas, recognition and advocacy for community colleges and community college leadership development, speak indirectly to open-door objectives, as well (AACC, 2006).

Three of AACC's affiliate councils focus on open-door issues: the National Council on Black American Affairs, the National Community College Hispanic Council, and the National Asian/Pacific Islander Council (AACC, 2009a). AACC works with foundation and university partners to lead the Achieving the Dream: Community Colleges Count initiative (Achieving the Dream [ATD], 2009), which now involves more than 85 community colleges across the nation. Modules of AACC's Leading Forward program, funded by the W. K. Kellogg Foundation, are designed to provide community college leaders with expertise on equity, diversity, and student success initiatives (AACC, 2009b). In addition, AACC is working with other organizations to promote the expansion of programs and services for older learners and people with disabilities.

The Lumina Foundation for Education

As a premier philanthropic, private, independent organization based in Indianapolis, Indiana, the Lumina Foundation for Education is guided by its belief that postsecondary education remains one of the most beneficial investments that individuals can make in themselves and that society can make in its people (Lumina Foundation, 2009). In its 2006 annual report, the Lumina Foundation stated that its primary objective is "to restore the United States' position as the global leader in educational attainment by the year 2025" (Lumina Foundation, 2006, p. 9). Today, the Lumina Foundation's work is reflected through three milestones of progress: student preparedness, student success, and college productivity. Throughout its history of supporting research initiatives, innovative programming, assessment and evaluative techniques, and the like, the Lumina Foundation is a pioneer of many national programs that help to erase the barriers to higher education that students face.

The Lumina Foundation strives to help people across the country achieve their full potential by increasing the accessibility and effectiveness of higher education. It offers tangible support for the community college open-door philosophy through its many projects, partnerships, research initiatives, and publications. With the importance of open and effective education as its focal point, the Lumina Foundation pursues its mission with a threefold approach: increasing access, ensuring success, and providing opportunities for adult learning. The foundation provides national leadership in addressing the varied barriers that impede traditionally underserved and underprepared groups from reaping the benefits of higher education. Foundation researchers suggest that many low-income youth aspire to attend college but might be deterred by psychological barriers resulting from many years of low expectations and little academic support or encouragement, which ultimately destroys self-confidence.

Another primary obstacle for underserved and underprepared populations, according to Lumina Foundation researchers, is the cost associated with higher education. The continued increase in college costs coupled with a lack of information about options for funding college attendance discourages many low-income students and their families from thinking of postsecondary education as a viable option. Misconceptions about managing the cost of higher education and the process of obtaining grants and loans have kept large numbers of otherwise academically prepared students from attending college.

Given the consequences of these obstacles, the Lumina Foundation recognizes that education and motivation must be driving forces to improve access, especially among students who lack information and have not been encouraged to pursue postsecondary education. In this regard, the foundation supports many publications such as the Lumina Foundation *Focus* magazine and *First in the Family*, a book written by and for first-generation college students (Cushman, 2005). This book provides real-life examples, experiences, and advice about what it takes to successfully pursue a college education. In addition, the Lumina Foundation seeks to improve student access and success through three major initiatives (ATD, KnowHow2GO, and Making Opportunity Affordable), as well as a host of other programs.

- Designed as a program to "help more college students succeed," ATD provides support to higher education institutions to assist underpresented populations of college students, particularly students of color and low income, to identify and overcome barriers to be successful (ATD, 2009).
- KnowHow2GO, launched in January 2007, targets low-income and first-generation students in grades 8–10, their parents, and other adults to encourage students to start the college preparation process early. A national multimedia and public service advertising campaign, KnowHow2GO is a joint effort between the Advertising Council, the Lumina Foundation for Education, and the

American Council on Education. The campaign features television and radio public service announcements, outdoor and print advertising, and an interactive Web site (www.KnowHow2GO.org; see also Ward, 2007).

- Directed by its mission as "an unprecedented effort to increase the number of college graduates within available resources while preserving instructional quality" (Lumina Foundation, 2008), the Making Opportunity Affordable initiative, financed by the Lumina Foundation, provides funding to states to increase the productivity of university and college education systems.
- The Transitions to College Project is a research-based undertaking that promotes successful high school–to–college transition strategies for low-income students (Social Science Research Council, 2009).
- The Gaining Early Awareness and Readiness for Undergraduate Programs (GEAR UP) initiative provides monetary support services to colleges that focus on middle- and high-school students by exposing them to the college experience through such services as campus visits, tutoring, and academic advising (U.S. Department of Education, 2009).
- College Goal Sunday brings professionals together to help low-income families apply for college financial aid (College Goal Sunday, 2009).

Recognizing that one of the most critical factors in determining success in college is the completion of a rigorous high school program, these education, motivation, and college recruitment programs are designed to have a substantial effect on high school completion and transition to community college. Building on that structure, the Lumina Foundation is playing a central national leadership role in advocating and supporting student success through the ATD initiative (ATD, 2009). The foundation has served as a pioneer of this national program, which is also supported by a number of other national associations, universities, and other foundations. ATD is an innovative national program focused on improving success among low-income and minority students at community colleges. The colleges involved in this initiative must develop a strong emphasis on data-based, continuous improvement of student success from developmental education courses to college-level courses to completion of certificates and associate degrees and transfer to baccalaureate institutions. The program focuses on closing the achievement gap between minority and low-income students and the general college population.

The League for Innovation in the Community College

The open-door philosophy of the comprehensive community college resonates through the League, whose directors are presidents and chancellors of member community colleges. The League is focusing on initiatives in eight areas: technology, learning, leadership, student success, workforce development, research and practice, resource development, and diversity and equity (League, 2009d).

The League's learning initiative relates directly to the open-door philosophy. A pioneer and advocate for the learning college concept, the League has long promoted the transformation of community colleges from teaching colleges to learning colleges, with a collegewide focus on increasing the outcomes of student learning. Given the varied learning styles represented in today's diverse student body, the League's research, publication, instructor and staff professional development, and model program development activities are having a positive effect on student success in community colleges. For example, the League's Learning College Project supports a network of colleges that showcase best practices for learning-centered institutions (League, 2009g).

The League's workforce development initiative includes the College and Career Transitions Initiatives (CCTI) (League, 2009a) and the Community College Workforce Partnership Network (League, 2009h). These initiatives have the objective of improving the college preparedness of students and facilitating the transition of students from high school to higher education and ultimately to the workforce, through partnerships with education, business, and government stakeholders.

The League's technology, student success, and diversity and equity initiatives encompass elements of student access, student success, and inclusiveness. These initiatives include the following:

- The Bridging the Digital Divide project addresses the disenfranchisement of those affected by the lack of access to technology by improving access and working to close the gap in technological skills among minority and low-income populations (League, 2009b).
- Keeping America's Promise outlines the current and future challenges facing the community college and encourages leadership dialogue to address these issues (League, 2009c).
- Remedial Education Implementation Project examines ways in which improved remedial education programs can help to ensure the success of underprepared community college students (League, 2009f).
- PLATO Research Project, a research-based study, aims to increase success in developmental mathematics through Internet-based courses (League, 2009e).

COMBASE

Driven by a "common interest in community-based education" (COMBASE, 2009), COMBASE was launched in 1974 by 10 community colleges. Today its membership of about sixty 2-year colleges is orchestrated by COMBASE's purpose to showcase exemplary practices and share expertise through various publications and networking avenues. COMBASE further underscores its efforts as established under its community-based education mission statements, performance-oriented education concepts, organizational development series, and its overall objectives to promote and provide awareness, understanding, support, and current information for institutional leaders.

Jobs for the Future

Jobs for the Future (JFF) is a nonprofit organization that promotes high-quality educational experiences for students and the empowerment of adults to achieve economic stability. It conducts research to identify and understand barriers to success, partners with other organizations to plan and implement projects, advocates for public policy that increases educational and economic opportunities for traditionally underserved populations, and offers consulting services to those seeking to reach these goals (JFF, 2009a). JFF encourages economic stability through promoting opportunities for adults to gain skills necessary to join the workforce and compete in a global economy. JFF also sponsors programs to provide individuals with opportunities to develop employability skills (JFF, 2009f). One such program, Breaking Through, is aimed directly at community colleges; it is designed to promote community college programs that enable undereducated adults to gain the skills and technical abilities necessary to successful careers (JFF, 2009b).

Improving the transition from youth to adulthood is another primary goal of JFF. The foundation recognizes that many high school graduates are not prepared for the transition and need support and encouragement to attain the postsecondary education that will provide them with increased economic security. To address this deficiency, JFF supports a number of initiatives:

- Bridging the Divide is a study of credit-based transition programs that facilitate the transition between high school and college by allowing students to earn college credit while still in high school. By collecting and analyzing data, JFF hopes to inform future policy decisions related to this promising approach to encouraging pursuit of postsecondary education (JFF, 2009c).
- Double the Numbers 2007 seeks to improve public policies that address barriers to higher education that young people face. It focuses on promoting access to education opportunities and success for those who might be underprepared for the challenges of postsecondary education (JFF, 2009d).
- Making Opportunity Affordable is a multifaceted project that addresses increasing access to educational opportunities, maintaining the quality of postsecondary education, and controlling the costs associated with college (JFF, 2009e).

Nellie Mae Education Foundation

Founded in 1998, the Nellie Mae Education Foundation (NMEF) promotes accessibility, quality, and effectiveness of education (NMEF, 2009). The NMEF mission is "to stimulate transformative change of public education systems across New England by growing a greater variety of higher quality educational opportunities that enable all learners–especially and essentially underserved learners–to obtain the skills, knowledge and supports necessary to become civically engaged, economically self-sufficient life-long learners" (NMEF, 2009). NMEF provides grants and technical assistance to programs and strategies focused on improving academic achievement and supporting underserved learners through five strategic initiatives: Early Learning, Time for Learning, Pathways to Higher Learning, Adult Learning, and Systems Building. As it recalibrated its strategic funding priorities in 2008, NMEF added another focus on increasing knowledge on how to significantly improve outcomes for learners in the New England region. Its use of the term *engaged grantmaking* allows NMEF to offer short-term and long-term funding options, provide support for organizational capacity by assessing readiness and interest, provide input from policy and educational stakeholders through its cluster concept of conversation and dialogue on the issues, and incorporate a two-tiered evaluation structure that assesses the progress of both the foundation and the grantee.

The Jack Kent Cooke Foundation

Jack Kent Cooke left most of his fortune to establish the Foundation (JKCF) in 2000, with the mission of helping young people of exceptional promise reach their full potential through education (JKCF, 2009a). The newspaper and cable television entrepreneur believed that most young people have a will to succeed, but for lack of opportunity, settle for less than their best. To close the financial gap experienced by students from low-income backgrounds, JKCF supports young people of exceptional promise, application, deportment, and character who have financial need and demonstrated excellence in academic endeavors and extracurricular activities (JKCF, 2009d). A few of the initiatives are the following:

- Community College Transfer initiative. This 5-year initiative seeks to increase opportunities for high-achieving, academically prepared, low- to moderate-income students to transfer to selective colleges and universities (JKCF, 2009b).
- College Access programs. JKCF's College Advising Corps has awarded eleven $1 million grants to state flagship universities and highly selective private institutions, aimed at substantially increasing college enrollment and graduation among low-income students in high schools and community colleges (JKCF, 2009c).
- Undergraduate Transfer Scholarship program. Each year, the JKCF awards approximately 50 scholarships to community college students who plan to transfer to 4-year colleges and universities (JKCF, 2009e).

A Partnership to Improve State-Level Student Success Data

The State Data Project: Helping Community Colleges Evaluate and Promote Student Success is a joint effort of the Ford Foundation's Bridges to Opportunity initiative and the ATD initiative to help states use data to improve outcomes for community college students and particularly for low-income adults (Douglas Gould and Company, 2009). To improve state-level educational policy and practices, states agencies and colleges must be able to track the progress of students at each level of education and into the labor market. Data will allow states and colleges to identify critical filter points at which many students drop out and use this information to determine what improved policies and practices are needed to empower students to advance to higher education and better jobs.

LEADERSHIP DEVELOPMENT AND THE OPEN DOOR

The need to cultivate 2-year college leaders who embrace the open-door philosophy is the impetus for programs that focus on community college leadership development. Designed to enhance existing competencies and increase awareness of critical issues, degree programs and national and regional leadership training institutes provide specialized exposure to research initiatives, mentoring, management, and planning. Several such programs are highlighted here.

The Community College Leadership Program of the University of Texas at Austin

The Community College Leadership Program is perhaps best known for the many community college presidents who are among its graduates. However, it has also provided national leadership for numerous research, publication, and application programs related to the community college open door (University of Texas, 2009). One such area of leadership seeks to increase the effectiveness of instructors and administrators in providing access and success for diverse students. Each year, large numbers of community college instructors and staff members attend a premier conference on community college teaching and learning sponsored by the leadership program, which has also led national efforts advocating improvements in developmental education and institutional effectiveness. Two current areas of national leadership are the Community College Survey of Student Engagement (2009) and ATD (2009). In the latter, the Community College Leadership Program partners with AACC, the Lumina Foundation, and other organizations to achieve increases in student academic achievement.

American Association of Women in Community Colleges and the National Leadership Development Institute

Another affiliate organization of AACC is the American Association of Women in Community Colleges (AAWCC). Regarded as the leading national organization that champions women and maximizes their potential, the mission of AAWCC emphasizes its dedication to "change women's lives through leadership and education, thus strengthening our colleges and communities" (AAWCC, 2004). Considered a premier program, the National Institute for Leadership Development (NILD, 2009), supported and advocated by AAWCC, focuses on preparing women for leadership positions in community colleges. In its 28 years, NILD has developed a national and international network of over 6,000 women leaders and who have developed their talents and excelled through networking and support gained as institute participants.

Future Leaders Institute

Further accentuating the need to cultivate future community college leaders, the Future Leaders Institute is directed to mid-level 2-year college administrators who are seeking to advance to higher leadership positions. This 5-day intensive seminar touches on topics such as institutional change; leadership style; motivating and team building; conflict resolution; understanding legal issues; use of technology and creating community through access, inclusion, and diversity (AACC, 2009b).

STUDENT DEVELOPMENT AND THE OPEN-DOOR MISSION

Under the auspices of student services, an important link to the open-door principle is reinforced through the inclusion of the student development philosophy specifically for 2-year colleges under leading national and international student affairs and student development organizations. Two flagship organizations are the American College Personnel Association (ACPA) and the National Association of Student Personnel Administrators (NASPA). Founded in 1924, ACPA is a "comprehensive student affairs association that advances student affairs and engages students for a lifetime of learning and discovery" (ACPAa, 2009). Headquartered in Washington, DC, it boasts a membership of more than 8,000 members that consist of entry-level to senior higher education administrators and officials, faculty, and graduate and undergraduate students enrolled in higher education programs.

ACPA's mission, vision, and core values each emphasize the needs of the student learner on diversity, inclusiveness, and outreach. Its creation of the Commission on Student Development in the Two-Year College allows ACPA to focus specifically on issues related to student development programs and practitioners in 2-year institutions. The commission promotes the enhancement of student development programs and professional development of student development personnel. It also acts as an advocate for student development programs and initiatives in 2-year institutions (ACPAb, 2009). The commission publishes a newsletter three times throughout the year that addresses student development and the community college.

NASPA was founded in December 1918. It is the voice for student affairs administration, policy, and practice, and it affirms the commitment of the student affairs profession to educating the whole student and integrating student life and learning.

Its 11,000 members are committed to serving college students by embracing NASPA's core values of diversity, learning, integrity, collaboration, access, service, fellowship, and the spirit of inquiry (NASPA, 2009). Recognizing that one of the most influential postsecondary educational communities in higher education is the 2-year college, NASPA created the Community Colleges Division to "provide within NASPA professional programs, activities, services and initiatives to further the growth of professionals working in community colleges at each level—entry, middle management, and senior student affairs professionals" (NASPA, 2009).

The leaders of NASPA understood that, by addressing the critical issues and needs of its constituents, it could augment its focus on contemporary leadership opportunities and foster innovative practices by creating a series of national centers, divisions, and academies that provide programs, services, and resources to promote excellence in higher education. The Community Colleges Division of NASPA underscores that importance and commitment to the open-door mission and is certainly a complement to the organization's longstanding tradition of supporting higher education leaders and solving student issues.

An affiliate organization of AACC, the National Council on Student Development (NCSD) also focuses on serving the needs of student development professionals in the community college. NCSD is regarded as the "nation's primary voice for sharing knowledge, expertise, professional development and student advocacy for community college student development practitioners and leaders" (NCSD, 2009). NCSD enables members to have a direct connection to AACC, provides leadership opportunities in student development, distributes information on student development trends and forecasts, supports social and workforce development for constituent communities, and focuses on the success of students through their development.

———◦◦◦———

All elements of the new open-door model of the community college—student access, student success, inclusiveness, and community engagement—are being supported by a powerful partnership of local community colleges, college consortia, state-level organizations, national associations, foundations, universities, business organizations, government units, and nonprofit agencies. Whereas local community colleges serve at the cutting edge of program and service delivery to individuals and groups at the grassroots level, state and national organizations take the big picture perspective by shaping public policy, developing future community college leaders, leading research and evaluation projects, and in other ways creating a state and national environment for the success of the local community colleges and students they serve. These local, state, and national organizations serve individuals by empowering all citizens to achieve their full career and academic potential, especially those who experience barriers to success due to low income, limited job and literacy skills, and other personal, family, or community factors. They also serve the public economic and civic good by ensuring that previously disenfranchised groups become contributing members of a globally competitive workforce and an integral part of community and national life. This partnership is indeed building an aristocracy of achievement based on a democracy of opportunity.

REFERENCES

Achieving the Dream. (2009). *About Achieving the Dream.* Retrieved from http://www.achievingthedream.org/aboutatd/default.tp

American Association of Community Colleges. (2006, August 4). *Mission statement.* Retrieved from http://webadmin.aacc.nche.edu/About/Pages/mission.aspx

American Association of Community Colleges. (2009a). *Affiliate councils.* Retrieved from http://webadmin.aacc.nche.edu/About/Pages/affiliatecouncil.aspx

American Association of Community Colleges (2009b). *Future Leaders Institute.* Retrieved from http://www.aacc.nche.edu/newsevents/Events/fli/Pages/default.aspx

American Association of Women in Community Colleges. (2004). *AAWCC mission statement.* Retrieved from http://data.memberclicks.com/site/aawcc/AAWCC_Mission_Statements.pdf

American College Personnel Association. (2009a). *About ACPA.* Retrieved from http://www2.myacpa.org/au/index.php

American College Personnel Association. (2009b). *Commission for student development in the two-year college.* Retrieved from http://www.myacpa.org/comm/twoyear/index.cfm

College Goal Sunday. (2009). *About us.* Retrieved from http://www.collegegoalsundayusa.org/about

COMBASE. (2009). *A cooperative for the advancement of community-based postsecondary education.* Retrieved from http://staff.bcc.edu/combase/info.html

Community College Survey of Student Engagement. (2009). *Overview.* Retrieved from http://www.ccsse.org/aboutccsse/aboutccsse.cfm

Cushman, K. (2005). *First in the family: Advice about college from first-generation students: Your high school years.* Providence, RI: Next Generation Press.

Douglas Gould and Company. (2009). *State Data Project: Helping community colleges evaluate and promote student success.* Retrieved from http://www.communitycollegecentral.org/Resources/research/StateDataProject/index.html

Jobs for the Future. (2009a). *About JFF.* Retrieved from http://www.jff.org/Content/About+JFF.html

Jobs for the Future. (2009b). *Breaking Through: Helping low-skilled adults enter and succeed in college and careers: Project description.* Retrieved from http://www.breakingthroughcc.org/

Jobs for the Future. (2009c). *Bridging the Divide: Blending secondary and post-*

secondary curricula into a coherent course of study. Retrieved from http://www.jff.org/Content/Current+Projects_Improving+Youth+Transitions_Bridging+the+Divide+.html

Jobs for the Future. (2009d). *Double the numbers 2007.* Retrieved from http://www.jff.org/Content/Current+Projects_Improving+Youth+Transitions_Double+the+Numbers+2007.html

Jobs for the Future. (2009e). *Making opportunity affordable.* Retrieved from http://www.jff.org/Content/Current+Projects_Improving+Youth+Transitions_Making+Opportunity+Affordable.html

Jobs for the Future: (2009f). *Projects.* Retrieved from http://www.jff.org/Content/Current+Projects.html

Jack Kent Cooke Foundation. (2009a). *About Jack Kent Cooke.* Retrieved from http://www.jkcf.org/about-jkcf/about-jack-kent-cooke/

Jack Kent Cooke Foundation. (2009b). *Community college transfer.* Retrieved from http://www.jkcf.org/grants/community-college-transfer/

Jack Kent Cooke Foundation. (2009c). *Grant recipients.* Retrieved from http://www.jkcf.org/grants/college-access/grant-recipients/

Jack Kent Cooke Foundation. (2009d). *Our mission.* Retrieved from http://www.jkcf.org/about-jkcf/our-mission/

Jack Kent Cooke Foundation. (2009e). *Undergraduate transfer scholarships.* Retrieved from http://www.jkcf.org/scholarships/undergraduate-transfer-scholarships/

League for Innovation in the Community College. (2009a). *About CCTI.* Retrieved from http://www.league.org/league/projects/ccti/index.html

League for Innovation in the Community College. (2009b). *Bridging the Digital Divide project.* Retrieved from http://www.league.org/league/projects/digital_divide.htm

League for Innovation in the Community College. (2009c). *Keeping America's promise.* Retrieved from http://www.league.org/league/projects/promise/index.html

League for Innovation in the Community College. (2009d). *League initiatives.* Retrieved from http://www.league.org/league/about/initiatives.htm

League for Innovation in the Community College. (2009e). *PLATO: Adding up the distance.* Retrieved from http://www.league.org/league/projects/plato_rproject.htm

League for Innovation in the Community College. (2009f). *Remedial Education Implementation project.* Retrieved from http://www.league.org/league/projects/remedial/index.htm

League for Innovation in the Community College. (2009g). *The Learning College project.* Retrieved from http://www.league.org/league/projects/lcp/index.htm

League for Innovation in the Community College. (2009h). *The Workforce Network.* Retrieved from http://www.league.org/league/projects/ccwpn/network.html

Lumina Foundation for Education. (2006). *The time is now* [Annual report]. Retrieved from http://www.luminafoundation.org/publications/2006AnnualReport.pdf

Lumina Foundation for Education. (2008). *Making Opportunity Affordable: Our mission*. Retrieved from http://www.makingopportunityaffordable.org/

Lumina Foundation for Education. (2009). *About us*. Retrieved from http://www.luminafoundation.org/

National Council on Student Development. (2009). *Mission*. Retrieved from http://www.ncsdonline.org/home/index.html

National Institute for Leadership Development. (2009). *The premier program developing women "leaders" in community colleges*. Retrieved from http://www.pc.maricopa.edu/nild/index.html

Nellie Mae Education Foundation. (2009). *Vision, mission and history*. Retrieved from http://www.nmefdn.org/Foundation/

Social Science Research Council. (2009). *Transitions to college: From theory to practice*. Retrieved from http://programs.ssrc.org/ki/Transitions/

University of Texas at Austin. (2009). *Community College Leadership Program: CCLP projects and initiative*. Retrieved from http://edadmin.edb.utexas.edu/cclp/initiatives.php

U.S. Department of Education. (2009). *Gaining early awareness and readiness for undergraduate programs* (GEAR UP). Retrieved from http://www.ed.gov/programs/gearup/index.html

Ward, D. (2007). The college access imperative requires financial and information resources. *Presidency, 10*(1), 5–6.

Index

Note. Page numbers followed by *t* indicate material in tables.

Aa

Kk

Ll

Mm

Nn

Pp

Pathways to Higher Learning initiative, 145
Pathways to the Future initiative, viii, 29
"people's college," 1
personal barriers, to success, 46, 47
PLATO Research Project, 143
"the poor college," 11
Portland Community College (Oregon),
35–36, 118
potential, opportunity to achieve full, 58
"Power of One," 45–46
preparedness, community college-secondary
school partnerships and, 34–38
President's Commission on Higher Education
for American Democracy, 2–3
procedural accommodations, for students
with disabilities, 19
Program in Course Redesign, 92–94, 97–98
Project SAIL, 90
The Prophet (Gibran), 77
public colleges, and return on investment,
71–73
public good, higher education as, 10
Public Law 94-142, 19

Qq

Quality Matters, 102

Rr

Raines, Max, 59
real data, decisions based on, 28–29
reciprocation, in community engagement, 71
recruitment of instructors, technology and,
101–103
reform, education, 126–128
Rehabilitation Act of 1973, 19
reinvention
career pathways and continuing
education, 123–137
open door, through national leadership,
139–149

remedial education. *See* developmental
education
Remedial Education Implementation Project,
143
return on investment (ROI), public colleges
and, 71–73
reverse transfer, 50–51
Rio Salado College (Arizona), 88, 93
Riverside Community College (California), 93
ROI. *See* return on investment
Rosenbaum, James, 127
Roueche, John, x
Roueche, Suanne, x

Ss

San Diego Community College District,
64–65
School to Work, 115
seat time, technology *vs.*, 99–100
Seattle Central Community College, 64
secondary schools
community college partnerships with,
34–38, 88
connections with, new levels of, 34
education reform and, 126–128
self-concept, weak, in at-risk students, 15–16
self-esteem, strengthening students', x
semantic-aware applications, 94
semiskilled workers, 110, 112
service learning, 52, 69–71
*Seven Principles of Good Practice in
Undergraduate Education* (Chickering
and Gamson), 91–92
shadowing, course, 102
Shaw, Ruth, 67
simulated testing, 90
Sloan-C Consortium, 90
SMART boards, 94
smart objects, 94
smart technology, 89, 94, 95
social benefit, of community engagement, 71
social entrepreneurship, 68
social networking, 10, 89
special needs programs, 20

diversity and sensitivity of, 63
qualified, and inclusiveness, 63
recruitment and development of,
technology and, 101–103
teacher education, 113, 129t
teaching
adapting new techniques of, 51–52
in career pathways model, 134t
and inclusiveness, 62
instructors' technological skills and,
101–103
next-generation technologies in, 89
technology, 87–105
aligning with mission and strategy, 103
appeal to today's students, 88–89
career cluster, 129t
and costs of instruction, 97–101
course redesign using, 92–94
in developmental education, 95–96
digital divide in access to, 103–104, 143
in instructor recruitment and
development, 101–103
learning theory and uses of, 91–92
Metcalfe's law and, 98–99
Moore's law and, 98
online resources on, 90
organizational impacts of, 97–103
student demand for, 97
in student services, 96–97
uses in postsecondary education, 89–91
and workforce education, 111–114, 116
Tech Prep, 115
Telepresence, 89
testing, simulated, 90
Time for Learning initiative, 145
Tough Choices or Tough Times (NCEE), 125
transfer
from community colleges. *See* university-
transfer programs
reverse, 50–51
transformation, evidence of, 9–10
transition, in education reform, 126–128
Transitions to College Project, 142
transportation, distribution, and logistics, 130t
Tri-County Technical College (South
Carolina), 35–36

TRIO, 35
Truman, Harry S., 2

Uu

Undergraduate Transfer Scholarship program,
145
underprepared students, 33–42
adult, interventions for, 39–42
advocacy for, 27–28
"cooling out" of aspirations, 127
customized approaches for, 41
education reform and, 126–128
secondary school, interventions for,
34–38, 41–42
in workforce education, 110, 116–117,
119
underserved, advocacy for, 27–28
United States Distance Learning Association,
90
university centers, at community colleges, 50
University of Cincinnati, 69
University of Maryland, 50
University of Texas at Austin, 146
University of Wisconsin, 50
university-transfer programs
improving, best practices for, 50–51
shift of younger students to, 9–10
as strategy for success, 49–51
workforce education *vs.*, 115
Upward Bound, 35

Vv
values, statement of, Wayne County
Community College District, 30
video
enhanced digital, 89
online, 90
video games, learning based on, 91
virtual classrooms, 89
Virtual Middle College, 88
vision statement, Wayne County Community
College District, 31
vocational education. *See* workforce
education

About the Contributors

John Bolden is executive vice chancellor of the Wayne County Community College District. Prior to being promoted to this position in 2006, he served as vice chancellor for student services. He earned his undergraduate and master's degrees in English at Wayne State University. During over 30 years of leadership in higher education, he has held positions in student services, adult education, developmental education, and disability services. He has been actively involved in state and regional efforts to improve academic support services, supplemental education, tutorial services, and developmental education.

Stephanie R. Bulger is vice chancellor of educational affairs at the Wayne County Community College District. Under her leadership, distance learning enrollment has grown dramatically, including among international students, high school students, and working professionals. She has focused on leading curricular innovation, faculty professional development, and assessment of student learning outcomes. Bulger is a consultant–evaluator and a distance education reviewer for the Higher Learning Commission of the North Central Association of Colleges and Schools and serves on the advisory board for the National University Telecommunications Network. She has distance learning experience in both the private and public sector, having served as a regional director for Thomson Learning. She holds a doctorate in higher education from the University of Michigan, where she received the 2000 Howard McClusky award.

Shawna J. Forbes is executive dean of instruction at the Wayne County Community College District (WCCCD). Among her duties are the coordination of adjunct faculty relations, student enrollment initiatives, relationships with regional high schools and other community organizations, and improvement of processes and procedures within the Division of Academic Affairs. Prior to serving as executive dean, Forbes held instructional leadership positions at the Downtown Campus of WCCCD. She holds an undergraduate degree in business administration from the Detroit College of Business, a master's degree in clinical psychology from the University of Detroit-Mercy, and is currently working on a doctoral degree at the University of Toledo.

Curtis L. Ivery has been chancellor of the Wayne County Community College District (WCCCD) since 1995. Prior to his tenure at WCCCD, he served as vice president for instruction at El Centro College and later at Mountain View College of the Dallas County Community College District. He started his academic career as a faculty member at West Texas State College and later served as a division chairperson at Westark Community College. Prior to moving to Dallas, he served as the commissioner of human services for the state of Arkansas and as a member of the cabinet of the governor of Arkansas. Ivery earned a doctorate in educational administration at the University of Arkansas. He has published over 400 articles as a newspaper columnist and is often called upon to be a commentator and speaker on urban and minority issues. His recently published book, *Journeys of Conscience,* contains a collection of essays about the richness and shortcomings of modern American culture. Ivery has provided leadership for national and state summits and conferences dealing with the urban crisis and the African American family. He has received a number of local, state, and national awards, including a 2002 "Michiganian of the Year" award by the *Detroit News* and the Southern Christian Leadership Conference's Outstanding Achievement in Higher Education award.

James Jacobs is the president of Macomb Community College (Michigan). At the national level, he has held leadership roles at the Community College Research Center at Columbia University. Jacobs specializes in occupational change and technology, economic development, workforce education, and retraining displaced workers. He has held leadership roles with the National Council on Workforce Education (NCWE) and as a coordinator of NCWE's Breaking Through initiative. He is on the National Advisory Board for the Manufacturing Extension Partnership program of the U.S. Department of Commerce. Jacobs is an editor of the *Journal of Career and Technical Education.* He has written several articles with a focus on career education in community colleges. He served on the advisory board of the National Assessment of Vocational Education. He serves as coordinator for the Achieving the Dream initiative at Wayne County Community College District. Jacobs earned his master's and doctoral degrees at Princeton University.

Gunder Myran is president emeritus of Washtenaw Community College (WCC), Ann Arbor, Michigan, having served as WCC's president for 23 years (1975 to 1998). For the past 8 years, he has served as a senior consultant to the chancellor of the Wayne County Community College District. Myran started his community college career at Jackson Community College (Michigan) as a faculty member and administrator and served as the chief instructional officer at Rockland Community College (New York). Prior to assuming the presidency at WCC, he served as an associate professor at Michigan State University (MSU), where he earned his doctorate. He co-led the MSU Kellogg Community College Community Services Leadership Program with Max Raines. Myran has published a number of books and articles on community college leadership, continuing education, and organizational strategy. He has served on the board of directors of the American Association of Community Colleges and as board chair for the National Council on Continuing Education and Training and the Michigan Community College Association. He received the Thomas J. Peters National Leadership Award from the Community College Leadership Program at the University of Texas, and national lifetime achievement and presidential leadership awards from the National Council for Continuing Education and Training. He was inducted into the international hall of fame of the Association for Higher Continuing Education in 2009.

Brian Singleton is executive dean in the Office of the Executive Vice Chancellor at the Wayne County Community College District (WCCCD). He assists the executive vice chancellor in developing and implementing strategic initiatives and grant-funded programs. Prior to his appointment as executive dean, he served at WCCCD as the dean of student services, associate dean for transfer programs, and assistant dean for career programs. Before joining the WCCCD staff, Singleton worked as an administrator for Detroit Public Schools. He earned a master's degree in business administration from the University of Phoenix and is currently working toward a doctoral degree at the University of Toledo.

George Swan is vice chancellor for campus operations at the Wayne County Community College District (WCCCD). He earned his master's and doctoral degrees at Wayne State University. Prior to joining the WCCCD staff in 1987, he held administrative positions at the Lewis College of Business and Wayne State University. Prior to his appointment as vice chancellor in 2006, he served at WCCCD as Eastern Campus president and in public relations positions. Swan serves on a number of national and local boards and is a consultant–evaluator for the Higher Learning Commission of the North Central Association of Colleges and Schools. He is recognized for his work in civic, cultural, and community development initiatives and is a frequent speaker and lecturer.

Laurance J. Warford is the senior workforce consultant and project director of the College and Career Transition Initiative and the Community College Workforce Partnership Network at the League for Innovation in the Community College. Prior to joining the League, he served as a community college liaison in the U.S. Department of Labor, as vice president for academic affairs at Lane Community College (Oregon), and as an administrator at Iowa Central Community College. Warford has served in national leadership roles with the National Council on Continuing Education and Training and is the author of a number of books and articles, including the 2006 *Pathways to Student Success* published by the League for Innovation in the Community College. He earned his doctoral degree from the University of Oregon and undergraduate and master's degrees from the University of Northern Iowa.

Debraha Watson is president of the Northwest Campus of the Wayne County Community College District (WCCCD), having served in other administrative roles at WCCCD beforehand. Before joining the WCCCD staff, she worked for over 30 years in the health industry, holding management positions for 25 years of that time. She is a registered respiratory therapist. She holds a doctorate in adult and higher education from Cappella University and master's degrees in adult and higher education (Morehead State University, Kentucky) and general administration (Central Michigan University).

Carol Wells leads the student services program of the Eastern Campus of the Wayne County Community College District (WCCCD). Prior to joining WCCCD in 2004, she held counseling and administrative positions at the University of Michigan-Dearborn. As the director of admissions and orientation there, she led Michigan's King-Chevez-Parks Initiative, which focuses on recruitment, scholarships, and retention of people of color. She served as president of the Michigan Association of Collegiate Registrars and Admissions Officers; in this position she worked to increase State of Michigan college scholarships for high school graduates.

Resources for the Community College Professional

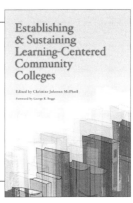